D1429072

THE SIX-FIGURE
JOB-HUNTING
HANDBOOK

The Six-Figure Job-Hunting Handbook

How to Replace Your $100,000+ Job

Glen Ellis
Jeff Jernigan

PRIMA VENTURE
An Imprint of Prima Publishing

Published by Prima Publishing, Roseville, California. Member of the Crown Publishing Group, a division of Random House, Inc., New York.

PRIMA VENTURE and colophon are trademarks of Random House, Inc. PRIMA PUBLISHING and colophon are trademarks of Random House, Inc., registered with the United States Patent and Trademark Office.

Interior figures by Michael Tanamachi

Library of Congress Cataloging-in-Publication Data
Ellis, Glen.
  The six-figure job-hunting handbook : how to replace your $100,000+ job / Glen Ellis, Jeff Jernigan.
    p. cm.
  Includes index.
  ISBN 0-7615-6372-5
  1. Job hunting I. Ellis, Glen. II. Title.
HF5382.7 J465 2002
650.14—dc21   2002074989

02 03 04 05 06 QQ 10 9 8 7 6 5 4 3 2 1
Printed in the United States of America

First Edition

Visit us online at www.primapublishing.com

The day came when I was ready for a career change. We also wanted to move across country. My wife, Dorothy, supported and encouraged me. I did the conventional things without success. Then I learned how to find the right job. But the key was making the commitment, drawing the line in the sand, and stepping across it. When I was discouraged and wanted to give up, she gave me a one-word answer that kept me going. The answer was "no." It was good advice then, and it's good advice now. Never give up.

—GLEN ELLIS

This book is for J. Walter Wallace, the consummate executive at 81 years of age who knows how to land on his feet. Husband, parent, businessman; Wally is my hero. His counsel is invaluable, his wisdom timeless, and his business decisions always put the company's interests first—without sacrificing the employees. This unique balance of a love for people and business savvy has influenced this book significantly, both through his example and his daughter, my wife, Nancy.

—JEFF JERNIGAN

CONTENTS

ACKNOWLEDGMENTS

We would like to thank the Prima team, especially David Richardson and Andrew Vallas, for their diligent application of talent to this work. Few editors are as professionally savvy or as easy to work with—an author's dream. For our clients whose experience has tailored, amended, and informed this book, we are grateful for your success and the part you have allowed us to play in your lives. Our friends and colleagues who have faithfully reviewed the early material and supplied gracious commentary and recommendations deserve acknowledgement as well. We deeply appreciate your influence in our lives on and off the page. Many professionals have influenced our careers over the last three decades in terms of both teaching us to search as well as teaching us the search business. Your influence is reflected here with our respect and gratitude. A special thanks to our agent. You took our idea, saw the potential and encouraged us to push ahead. You kept us focused on this task when other responsibilities pulled us away and you kept the communication going between us and the great people at Prima Publishing. We would like to acknowledge all those reading this book, anticipating a job transition or in the midst of one; you are the soldiers fighting the very real battles on the front lines of six-figure employment. We salute you!

INTRODUCTION

C areer transitions are difficult passages whether the job seeker is simply dissatisfied with his or her current position or has suddenly lost the job. At any given time in the United States, it is estimated that 23 million adults find themselves in one of these two categories. There are really two challenges here—the competition and the process.

Needless to say, if you are one of those 23 million people, you face stiff competition in the labor market as you try to make a change. Finding a new job is not just about finding a different place to earn an income; it is about one more piece in your career. Finding the right next job to further your career is absolutely critical for the short term *and* the long term because, like a chess game, this move will position you for the next move. The decision you make this time will impact your career forever, so it's important to do it right.

Even more challenging is the process. In all likelihood you are probably not very good at it. When was the last time you looked for a new job? You've been too busy working to concern yourself with the next job. Most people get pretty good at the work they do because they focus on it day after day. Then—often suddenly—they find themselves in the position of looking for a job. This is new territory for them and they don't have a handbook.

And that's what this book is all about. It's a guide to walk you through the entire process of what we like to call a "career transition." We start by looking at the process leading up to the need for finding a new job, whether it's a matter of a bad fit where you are now or a matter of being laid off. We recognize and deal with the intense emotions that result from this transition and deal with the fundamental issues of character that the search process reveals. Then we walk you through your own customized, step-by-step process of finding that next "right" job.

No longer a matter of answering newspaper ads and sending off resumes with a great cover letter, employment is now e-commerce. Hard-copy resumes do not usually change hands until the job seeker is face to face with the employer. Digital resumes have replaced expensive letterhead. E-mail has replaced the cover letter. Web pages have replaced the portfolio. Of all the tools in the job seeker's toolbox, the telephone and the Internet have risen to the top.

What's more, 83 percent of today's college graduates are already Internet savvy. They enter the job market far better equipped for the race than most of the job seekers that have gone on before them who are probably less savvy. Competing for the same job, those with the most savvy survive! The race is still an intelligent numbers game involving canvassing, personal marketing, sales, and negotiation, but the rules have changed. This is especially true where the hidden job market is concerned.

Although there are a lot of similarities in finding any new job, we are all put together differently and consequently have different needs and different abilities. We can guide you through the process but you have to do the work. Fortunately, when you've done the work this time, you will know how to do it the next time. And yes, there will be a next time. We live in a world where rapidly changing business realities can make jobs appear and disappear almost in the blink of an eye. The definition of workplace loyalty has changed. Employers are looking for contribution, and employees are looking for investment in their own development. This means neither one is necessarily committed to longevity. We can sit around and complain about this, or we can accept this reality and be prepared. If, in fact, you are prepared, you will be a better employee in your present job and you will be prepared for that next new career move when the time comes.

Getting ready to do it all over again is the last matter we deal with in this book. What you do today can provide valuable resources for that future job-seeking experience. Make every day count. Take the time to record your accomplishments and stay in touch with your network.

Your experience in a career transition won't be exactly like anyone else's. But you can bet that some of your experiences will be the same. Take heart! Others have gone before you! By understanding who you are—your strengths and weaknesses, your emotions and today's job-seeking realities—you can shorten your job search and become a life-long learner in the process.

Best of all, you increase your chances of finding the next right job that positions you for your future. It can be fun and rewarding. Enjoy the journey.

The Six-Figure
Job-Hunting
Handbook

CHAPTER 1

WHERE TO BEGIN?

This book has been written to provide guidelines for finding the highly compensated job. The first step in acquiring a new job is the realization that you need one. Chances are, you have already taken this first step or you probably wouldn't be reading this book. Your responses upon realizing you needed to look for a job may have run the gamut—ranging from shock to anger to fear to excitement and even to exhilaration. Whatever you may be experiencing right now, it is important to harness that energy and use the drive to motivate yourself to get started. Don't take a month off to get your thoughts together or sort your papers. You can do that later—right now, the more quickly you get started, the sooner you will get results. You may be replacing a job that has been lost, you may be moving on in your career, you may be moving up to a six-figure job for the first time—whatever your situation, the rules for finding the job are the same. And your previous work experience will contribute to your accomplishing this goal.

So, what is your situation? One scenario is that you have been laid off—or downsized or right-sized—right out of a position, perhaps one you have been performing successfully for many years. In today's economy and resulting work-world, such a scenario is not unusual. And even though the knowledge that you're not alone can give you some comfort, it can't change your reality—that you need to find another job. And in many cases, you need to find it fast.

A second scenario is that you "see the handwriting on the wall"—you know it's time to make a change. Perhaps you see that profits are going down, or maybe it's just an unstable environment. I just received a telephone call from a highly placed executive who is seeing the handwriting right now. He has a good job and is successfully performing it with demonstrable results. But he sees the dysfunctional management that he reports to and recognizes that his situation could change at any moment. This executive is wisely updating his resume and reenergizing his network while he still has a good job.

As in all of life's ventures, there are tradeoffs when you are looking for a new job. Many say it's best to be looking while you still have a job because it demonstrates that you are employable, but time and privacy limitations definitely constrict your search. On the other hand, when you don't have a job you have a lot of time to spend on the search and you can tell everyone that you are looking. So, whatever your lot in life, you have to find the advantages and take advantage of them.

What You Will Learn

This book will walk you, step-by-step, through the entire process of finding a new job. It may seem like a daunting task at this point. And, in truth, it *is* a big task to find a great job—but like all the other things you have accomplished in your life, there is a logical and systematic way to approach this task. And many of the chapters also contain a "Signing Bonus" or two, additional material to help you jump-start your job search.

How to Use This Book

In chapter 2, "The Career Mentality," we address the feelings and emotions that any job seeker experiences—how to recognize them, name them, and deal with them. We go on to explore the tremendous advancements in job search technology, then identify the five key elements of market penetration.

Clearly defining your career, clarifying your motivation, and understanding how you define success become critical in the completion of your job search. In a Signing Bonus in chapter 2, a definition of career is laid out for your consideration.

In chapter 3, "A Long Look in the Mirror," we address the important issue of where you are right now. Through a series of self-assessment inventories, you are led to a better understanding of who you are, what you have done, what is unique about you, what opportunity is ideal for you, what compensation you should expect, and what geographical limitations make sense for you.

A Signing Bonus in chapter 3 offers some important considerations if you are between positions and specifically asks, "Why think of yourself as unemployed?"

All this information is critical to putting together your selling document—your resume. In chapter 4, "Marketing Yourself," we address the most fundamental question of all: What is the purpose of your resume? Then we provide detailed descriptions of resume types and help you construct yours. We also describe the various ways you can distribute your information.

Chapter 4 also covers the cover letter. Suffice it to say here: So important is the cover letter that you should *never* send a resume without one.

In order to get the important things done in the work of seeking employment, you must plan ahead, be organized, and use your time efficiently. Chapter 5, "Planning for Success," helps you set up the systems that will allow you to work effectively and consistently for however long it may take to accomplish your goal. And remember: This project is just like a lot of other projects you have done in that about 20 percent of what you do gives you 80 percent of the results. So understand what tasks are important and be sure you do those first.

By now, you are ready for the answer to the question that's been burning inside you: Where are the jobs? The simple answer is that at least 80 percent of them are "hidden," and in the case of six-figure positions for the executive, the figure is probably closer to 100 percent.

Before you throw up your hands in despair and drop this book, be assured that there is a very good process for uncovering the hidden jobs. In chapter 6, "The Hidden Job Market," we show you how to find opportunities. Like a gold prospector of earlier years, you learn how to search out likely veins of productive ore, how to extract samples, how to assay their value, and, finally, how to excavate the gold ore. And as with any raw ore, the amount of true gold is small, so chapter 6 also shows you how to refine the ore to find that one nugget you're looking for.

The heart of this book is chapter 7, "The Art of Networking." If you could do only one thing in a job search, this is what you would want to do. And by the time you have worked through the early chapters in this book, you will be ready to accept the challenge of perfecting your networking skills. In fact, if you can step outside the urgency of getting a job, you may find that networking is an enjoyable process and that it opens doors you never knew existed. Indeed, this one skill may revolutionize your business life for the rest of your career.

The Signing Bonus for chapter 7 suggests an important way to use the Internet for research: using online booksellers to increase your contacts. Don't miss this technique—you'll be able to incorporate this into your business life for years to come.

Once you have the networking process down, you will find yourself in front of people who have the authority to hire you. In chapter 8, "Relational Selling," we discuss the importance of this technique and how to become effective at it. Yes, this is selling. *And it is your most important product—yourself.* We'll explore how to communicate with high-level decision makers, the sales cycle, how to work with recruiters and employers, how to get an interview, and what to do when you do get an interview.

At some point, you *will* receive an offer. That is the event you are waiting and working for, and it is important that you do your homework early enough and thoroughly enough to be ready to negotiate when the time comes. Chapter 9, "Executive Compensation," addresses relocation packages, stock options, merit programs, legal issues, taxes, and other such issues.

By the time you have done the work to become an effective job seeker and found that great six-figure job, you will be eager to begin work. That's great, and it's exactly how it should be. However, there is one more important point to consider—you probably will have to do this again sometime.

With that possibility in mind, we offer chapter 10, "Pursuing Your Career." You've often heard the old expression "use it or lose it." This is as true with job search skills as with any other skill. So we urge you to follow through on the steps in chapter 10—doing so will position you for the next time you are a job seeker.

Years ago I reached a point in my career where I wanted a change. We lived in Michigan but for 16 years had wanted to be in Seattle. We made several unsuccessful attempts to relocate. Our children were getting older, and we realized that if we didn't relocate soon we would never be able to and would lose our dream.

I was teaching at the time, and at the end of the school year I got in my car and headed toward Seattle. Before I pulled out of the driveway I told my wife, "I'm not coming back until I get a new job." That was quite a boast. And even though I didn't really know what I was saying, it was in reality exactly the commitment I needed to make in order to accomplish my goal.

I arrived in Seattle and spent three weeks doing the things we recommend in this book. During those three weeks, I had 72 information interviews and one of them led to a new job. Because I followed the system and didn't give up, I was able to change geography, change careers, and significantly increase my compensation. Now, we can't promise that will happen for everybody—and if you can improve on your current career, in any way, that is a great accomplishment—but we *can* guarantee that if you don't do something, nothing will ever change.

Both of us have hammered out the principles in this book in the crucible of our own experience. More important, we have tested the advice through the lives and careers of those we have coached and placed in career-expanding roles over more than 50 years of combined experience. Given total commitment and a realistic understanding of the work and time involved, it has worked every time. Your experience in delving into this book and implementing what you find here is like a journey. And your journey will be unique, just like everyone's is.

Because it is unique, no promises can be made. You are the captain of your vessel, charting your own course. In the process of the journey, you will find that we encourage you to deal with the whole person. If you are reluctant to deal with who you are and the real contributions and gifts you bring to the workplace, you will find the advice given here less effective. You are a special person. You are not defined by the work you do but by the difference you make because of those unique attributes that reflect who you really are—valuable in every sense of the word.

Enjoy the journey and hang on for the ride!

CHAPTER 2

THE CAREER MENTALITY

C areer transitions are difficult passages whether you simply are dissatisfied with your current position or you have suddenly lost a job. It is estimated that at any given time in the United States there are 23 million adults who find themselves in one of these two categories. And regardless of the category they fall in, they face two main challenges: the competition and the process.

If you are one of those 23 million people, you face stiff competition in the labor market as you try to make a change. Finding a new job is not just about finding a different place to earn an income; it is about one more piece in your career. Finding the right next job to further your career is absolutely critical for the short term *and* the long term. It's like a chess game—this move positions you for the next move. The decision you make this time will impact your career forever, so it's important to do it right.

Even more challenging than the competition, however, is the process. In all likelihood, you are not very
good at it. When was the last time you looked for a job
that pays six figures? You're too busy doing your present
job to concern yourself with the next job. Then, often
suddenly, you find yourself in the position of job seeker.
This is new territory.

THE EXECUTIVE'S DILEMMA

None of us are immune to what comes our way each day,
whether expected or unexpected. When things happen to
us—or don't happen to us—in the way we anticipated,
we have feelings about the situation. When I lost my job
as a highly paid executive, it was without warning. My
first reactions were disbelief and denial—disbelief that
as a successful executive, I could be at risk for my job
just drying up and blowing away, and denial that I once
again had to compete in the real world for a top-notch
position. Oh, yes, there was also naïveté—I assumed
someone would snatch me up immediately just because I
was talented.

These are just some of the psychological challenges
executives face in the beginning. Shedding these feelings
and getting beyond them is helped by a humorous dose
of reality early in the search process. If some of the following experiences have not happened to you yet, just
give it time.

A recruiter or employer calls you, excited about your
availability. You have a great conversation, maybe
you're even asked to send additional material. Then
you don't hear anything. Ever. They don't even ex-
tend the courtesy of returning your calls or e-mails.

You spend the entire day trying to contact people
and can't get through to anyone.

Checking your posted Web sites, you discover your resume has vanished.

While crawling around on the floor, your one-year-old grandson—or two-year-old daughter or other similar danger in your life—found and tore to bits your list of user IDs and passwords, the list you need in order to access your Internet information on two dozen sites, the one you don't keep on your computer or have an extra copy of.

Your computer crashes, taking you offline for two whole days.

A power failure wipes out the telephone system for an entire afternoon.

At the end of the day, you realize your resume wasn't attached to a single e-mail you sent out that day.

An unkind recruiter tells you that your resume stinks, that you are overreaching in exaggerating your qualifications, and that you know you are over-reaching.

A job description you respond to reads like it was made for you, but you never hear a word from anyone, not even to confirm they received your resume.

For the third time in a week, someone says to you, "Your resume is great! I wish we had it sooner! We just made an offer to someone else!"

You are running out of money and still don't have a job.

After eight hours at the computer, you don't have a single new lead of any kind.

It seems the only calls you get about a job are from people offering pyramid schemes, 100 percent commission sales positions, schemes to set you up as a work-at-home "professional," or various positions in various types of insurance.

SIGNING BONUS: PATIENCE

In my recent check of employment Web sites, it was clear that patience is not a virtue shared by many. One site was dedicated to a specific industry niche and had a chat room. While I was visiting the chat room as an uninvolved reader, someone logged on with a complaint. He had been looking for work in this particular niche for six months, had had six interviews in the first three months and nothing since. His plea was for leads, help, some words of wisdom, encouragement, anything to let a little daylight into his darkening world. Over the next 23 minutes, 41 other job seekers logged on.

Some had similar experiences to relate, some provided leads, others provided encouragement, the majority of them were equally frustrated. It is difficult to say if they had an effective search plan in place or not, or if they were playing the intelligent numbers game well.

It was easy to spot a common theme in their commiseration, though: impatience. To a person they were all impatient with the process. Patience is a key ingredient in taking the ups and downs out of the search process, but it is hard to come by when you are dealing with so many unknowns.

The more perspective you have, the better your understanding of the process, and the more completely you are informed, the easier patience becomes. Enduring patience isn't blind, and it has a foundation made up of many components.

- A good search plan
- Current knowledge of the status of employment in your targeted industries
- Confident understanding of what your primary arena of contribution is

- Confirmation that your marketing material represents you well
- Knowing that you are playing the numbers game intelligently
- A sense of being in touch with what is happening in and around you
- Regular communication with your network
- Encouragement and accountability provided by a confidant
- Solid research on targeted companies
- A track record of full days spent working your plan
- Proven skill in using your Internet tools
- A search system that automatically produces leads for you
- Family and friends that support you in your search efforts
- A solid track record of following up on employers and recruiters who asked you to stay in touch
- Documentation that allows you to monitor progress and trends in order to adjust your search plans appropriately
- Interview skills that have demonstrated their effectiveness even if a job offer did not result
- Intact social connections, enough rest, a good diet, and exercise
- A positive attitude
- A sense of humor

None of these elements by themselves make patience any easier, but if they characterize and undergird your search efforts, how much easier patience is than if you were working in the dark. The fewer unknowns you face, the easier patience comes.

The only other kind of call you get is from telemarketers who want your money. They only call right at the moment you're expecting to hear from a potential employer. Of course, the employer never calls.

The car needs an expensive repair, and at the same time, you need dental work and have to pay the dentist out of pocket because to save money, you opted not to continue your dental coverage.

Kind friends say when they bump into you, "Oh, you haven't found work yet?"

Your nonworking spouse lands a job using the targeted-company list you developed.

After five interviews with a company over six weeks, including two interviews they flew you out for, they make an offer to someone else.

Your neighbor comes home suddenly unemployed— and finds a job in two weeks. You've been looking for twelve.

The printer jams repeatedly. It eats almost an entire ream of paper before the problem is solved.

You buy the wrong software and have to take it back. Only, it was on sale and is not returnable.

Of all the executives laid off in your company when you were, you are the only one still hanging out there.

A recruiter tells you in a screening interview that you are overqualified but that they are going to submit your resume anyway. In your telephone interview with the employer, the employer tells you that you are underqualified.

You realize a day after sending it that your super-supreme cover letter contained seven grammatical and spelling errors.

Traffic is stacked up on the freeway, making you late for an interview. You call, and they tell you to come anyway. When you get there, the person you had an interview with is gone.

You successfully beat out the competition only to be told the position has been put on hold.

The answering machine cuts off before you can identify how to contact the excited recruiter who just described the perfect job and said, "You can reach me at—"

An employer calls and says, "You are our leading candidate. However, we are not considering relocation since we have a number of somewhat qualified local candidates."

The cover letter with attached resume that you sent to the e-mail address on a recruiter inquiry bounces back with the auto reply "unknown address."

An employer tells you when you check back at their invitation, "We were *this close* to making you an offer, but a candidate with better qualifications came along."

Don't think for a minute these things can't happen to you. In fact, *all* of these things happened to the same job seeker over a 14-week period of time. And it is very likely you will have your own novel experiences to add to the list.

In reality, less than 10 percent of the work you do to find a job will ever pay off. The problem is that you don't know which 10 percent is going to be effective, so you have to do all 100 percent of the work—day in and day out. The same mental toughness that helped make you a successful, highly paid executive is what is needed now. The dilemma you face is in part psychological. You have to first sell yourself on you.

Emotions are like the lights on the dashboard of your car. Some just give information (door open). Some

issue warnings (engine overheating). Some give you noti-
fication (left taillight out); some, illumination (overhead
reading light). Of all those lights, the ones we really pay
attention to are the warning lights.

Warning lights tell us there is something going on
under the hood that needs immediate attention. Some
emotions are like that. They can signal that something
is going on under our hood that we need to pay attention
to. When the engine temperature light glows red, we
don't ignore it—we don't cover it up with tape and think
the problem is solved just because we don't see the light
anymore. So why do we ignore the signals our feelings
are sending, when it really is the best opportunity we
have to peel the layers back and discover things about
ourselves (some may even be things we don't want recruiters or employers to discover)?

No, this is not an insinuation that something evil
lurks below. Those you interview with will be attuned to
your energy, your enthusiasm, and your confidence, as
well as to how you respond under pressure, your ability
to communicate without rambling, your demeanor, and
more. Many times, the interview will be structured
specifically to evaluate these things.

Here is the challenge: Most of these attributes can't
be faked. Your emotions drive many of these responses. If
you come across as euphoric (an "up") or depressed (a
"down") even a little bit, it could compromise the interview. So understanding and dealing with the roots of
your feelings about being a job seeker better prepares
you to have an interview that is genuine, couched in a
confident sincerity that invites their confidence in return.

And getting at the roots of your feelings does not
mean digging into how you feel about your mother or if
you are afraid of the dark. There are just a few simple
things to understand about yourself that will help you to
better manage your emotions so that they do not manage you at the wrong time. This is not about controlling

emotions by suppressing or repressing how you feel. It is about presenting yourself as a mature job seeker.

We are put together like an onion: in layers. Figure 2.1 depicts the layers.

Emotions don't arise out of thin air. Something drives them. Often we are very aware of what produced our feelings. At other times, we experience them as spontaneous even though they are not. The key to understanding them is a little self-examination. Ask yourself: What is the source of this feeling? What does it tell me is going on under the hood? Will others pick up on this feeling in an interview? Is it something positive I want them to see (excitement, enthusiasm, confidence) or is it something negative (discouragement, arrogance, anger)?

When you identify the source of your feelings, you are in a better position to adjust them appropriately and manage how they affect your demeanor and behavior. It is not necessary to memorize the Behavioral Response Levels. Figure 2.1 merely points out that emotions give

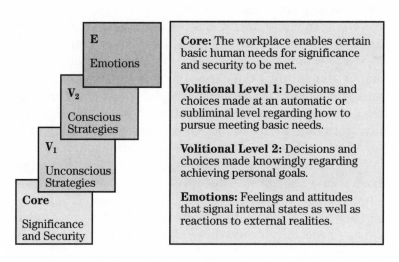

FIGURE 2.1: Behavioral Response Levels

us *and others* clues about how we respond to people and circumstances. Knowledge is power—in this case, power to give a good first impression on the telephone or in person. *You* must be sold on yourself—on your qualifications, your ability to do the job, the contributions you know you can make—in order for your audience to be sold.

If you don't peel back the layers, then you will either suppress or repress your feelings—but they will eventually leak out for others to see anyway. The goal is an *appropriate* transparency and vulnerability, even about your feelings. Being transparent first with ourselves enables us to decide how transparent to be, if at all, with others.

There are other challenges to face in the beginning as well. Most of the senior executives I have helped have been of an age that they can remember the days before computers proliferated on the business landscape. Certainly, they all have become computer savvy and have learned to navigate the digital landscape. But, like me, the skills developed were job-specific. There were holes in their skill set that were quickly revealed when they needed to master the art of networking in the Internet age. This is a technical dilemma.

No longer a matter of answering newspaper ads and sending off resumes with a great cover letter, employment is now e-commerce. Hard-copy resumes do not usually change hands until the executive is face-to-face with the employer. Digital resumes have replaced expensive letterhead. E-mail has replaced the cover letter. Web pages have replaced the portfolio. Of all the tools in your toolbox, the telephone and the Internet will rise to the top.

In competing for the same job, those who have the most savvy survive! The race is still an intelligent numbers game involving canvassing, personal marketing, sales, and negotiation—but the rules have changed. This is especially true where the hidden job market is concerned.

Developing that winning attitude about yourself and taking the time to master the technology you will be using puts you in the best position to understand the marketing process. There are five steps to consider: Find, Qualify, Win Acceptance, Close, and Negotiate.

1. Find: This is a canvassing process that is designed to identify opportunities you are a likely candidate for. It involves networking, responding to Web postings and other advertised opportunities, sifting through professional journals and trade association publications, contacting recruiters and employers, and engaging in whatever other activities put you in touch with the labor market.

2. Qualify: Not every opportunity you turn up will be right for you. To qualify opportunities, you need to research companies, discuss opportunities with recruiters, ask your network for information—in general, gather as much information as you can. This is especially necessary to do with the hidden job market: An executive opportunity that a search firm is actively seeking to fill comes with a lot of basic information to help you decide if you should pursue it, but no such help is available for non-advertised positions because no one is actively trying to sell those positions.

3. Win Acceptance: At some point you will target specific opportunities and begin the process of selling yourself. This may involve communicating with recruiters and with executives in the companies. The goal is to gain the active interest of decision makers. Ultimately, you may talk to several people inside and outside the company before you get the conversation you want with the individual empowered to hire you. You must win acceptance at each step along the way.

4. Close: The result you want is a job offer. This will not occur until you have jumped through all the hoops and passed all the interviews, satisfying the employer that you are the best choice for the position. In effect, you close the deal with each person you talk to with increasing stakes. The recruiter is sold on you and passes you on to the organization. The internal recruiter is sold on you and passes you on to the executive team. The executive team is sold on you and passes you on to the CEO or the board if you are potentially the next CEO. Each conversation is an opportunity to "close," and each requires a slightly different approach.

5. Negotiate: Once the offer is made it is not all over. There are a number of issues to be clarified, arrangements to be agreed upon, and details to be worked out. A major corporate client lost two candidates in a row during the process of negotiation. In one case, the candidate opted out, and in the other, the organization decided the candidate was not the one they wanted after all.

These marketing elements will be described as a single process later in this book. They were broken down here to make a point: As you work to penetrate the executive labor market you will be involved in all of these activities simultaneously. You will have several candidacies in the works at any given time, each at a different point in the process. You need to keep good records of where you are in the process with each opportunity. Otherwise, you will forget what you said to whom, what the next step is, and whether you should be winning acceptance or closing. Once you turn an initial contact into a solid opportunity, set up a separate file on the employer and keep notes on your progress. Review your notes to determine your goals, then plan your next conversation or other action accordingly.

DEFINING YOUR CAREER

Have you ever wondered what it would be like to enjoy your work so much that you are mildly surprised when people pay you? Looking back, can you see that what you do is more than the job you have and that the work themes that energize you have a common refrain? In every job you have had, including the one you may have now, does your sense of satisfied contribution center on the same functions time and again? Your career is defined by the unique impact you bring to everything you do in any job you have. This is because your career is not just a job.

Most successful executives haven't thought much about this. We just sort of float along, moving up in organizations or responding to opportunities to be recruited away. Our experience certainly is excellent, and the skills we pick up along the way certainly are consistent with the direction of our career. But for many of us, that career has been a matter of happenstance. We just happened to fall into something we liked and took the path of least resistance over the years.

There are many executives, however, who progress with purpose. Each job choice along the way is intentional, designed to help them keep learning and growing in their chosen profession. Who their employer is never seems important as long as they are improving. More important, they never think about alternative industries and the potential for a better fit in life. After all, they made this career choice years ago, and sure, things have changed since then, but why consider alternatives if things are working well?

A career is the sum of the activities and the relationships in our world of work that give meaning and purpose to what we do as the years go by. Job descriptions and titles won't do that. We are designed to work and to find fulfillment in work. The job simply acts like a parenthesis in our career continuum, giving temporary definition to our role. You may have many jobs in a lifetime but only one career. We often hear candidates say, "In my career, I have . . ." and enumerate the many different experiences and accomplishments a number of jobs have

---

SIGNING BONUS: WHAT IS A CAREER?

A career is not simply a job. As an executive, you need to consider seven basic elements that define your career as you prepare to take the next step.

1. A career is the fit between you and the work you do.
2. A career is the work you do that results in satisfaction.
3. A career is the accumulation of prior choices, each with its own weight and direction.
4. A career is a long-term development cycle.
5. A career is a process of constant adaptation.
6. A career consists of many relationships.
7. A career is a life direction.

---

provided them. Without realizing it, they are expressing something fundamental—one career, many jobs.

Perhaps you have found that niche or avenue in which your talents, gifts, skills, temperament, personality, and experience bear the most fruit. If so, that career needs to be nurtured. Like anything dynamic and growing, a career needs nurturing to remain alive and healthy. If you have not found that groove yet, it is high time to get on with the process of figuring it out. The first step is to learn who you are and what you can do so well that you are a natural and hardly aware you are doing anything at all. Without this fundamental understanding you will always be looking for a career and only finding jobs. A good career is the stuff dreams are made of.

It begins with playing an intelligent numbers game. Let's take the worst-case scenario—someone unexpectedly out of work who needs a job. On the average, executives looking for a job are going to make at least 700 contacts before they find what they are looking for. The "700 Rule" shouldn't be used as a yardstick to measure your progress, however tempting that may be. No, it's just a simple statistic on the sheer volume of work involved in sifting through the opportunities, getting your foot in the door, and landing just the right job. It means you have to work hard and long; you have to make finding a position your job every day, 8:00 A.M. to 5:00 P.M., day after day.

Figure 2.2 illustrates an actual recent executive job search.

Finding a job is a process, not an event. If your search has been structured properly, you can expect one callback for every 100 contacts with recruiters, employers, and referrals. For every three callbacks, you can expect to average one actual job interview. Usually, one out of five job interviews goes further, often far enough to result in an offer that you may or may not accept.

So you see, it is an intelligent numbers game—one offer letter requires 1,500 contacts that result in 15 callbacks that produce five actual interviews. Of course, words like *average, general,* and *approximate* are usually referring to a middle value in a wide range of figures that reflects the experience of a lot of people and that may not reflect your own. Some people get an offer after their first telephone call, some take months.

Now, assuming you have a targeted search plan and are not broadcasting your resume indiscriminately throughout the world, this process can be accelerated using some tricks of the trade, cutting the 1,500 count to around 700. A resume crafted to get the right kind of attention quickly, networking, carefully planned and timed follow-up, and discipline all help to winnow the chaff from the real opportunities and increase your odds of connecting with the right person at the right time, hence the reference to 700 contacts as an average.

Activity	Week 1	Week 2	Week 3	Week 4	Week 5	Week 6	Week 7	Week 8	Week 9	Week 10	Totals
Job Applications	22	13	18	9	15	10	28	19	15	20	169
Recruiter Contacts	20	26	15	8	10	8	31	29	4	5	156
Recruiter Interviews	0	5	2	0	2	2	0	2	2	1	16
Web Sites Posted	21	7	6	5	4	6	4	3	1	1	58
Networking	11	7	9	13	15	14	9	17	10	6	111
Employer Interviews	0	1	1	1	1	1	1	2	2	2	12
Blast Replies	0	387	0	0	0	186	0	0	0	0	573
	74	446	51	36	47	227	73	72	34	35	1095

FIGURE 2.2: Search Activity Statistics

The pie charts in figure 2.3 illustrate the impact of a targeted plan based on the preceding table and identify some of the Internet tools that help cut the numbers down.

Think of it as fishing. You know where the fish are most likely to be found. You have the right tackle and bait and you cast a very, very big net to snare the few opportunities that really interest you. There are a number of industries that can use your skills, and your targeted search should include multiple industries. Obviously, there may be more opportunities in one industry sector than another. However, the fewer contacts you make anywhere, the fewer job opportunities you'll snare in your net. You have to cast a big net to catch the right fish. Figure 2.4, Casting the Net, demonstrates this principle. With only 200 contacts you will uncover only one opportunity, and others are competing for that same job. With 800 contacts, you may uncover as many as 18 opportunities!

If you limit your search to the industry sector you are most familiar with, you may find only a few opportunities. Sector one contains only six; sector two only eight, and sector three only four jobs. Let's assume you are a computer professional with manufacturing and

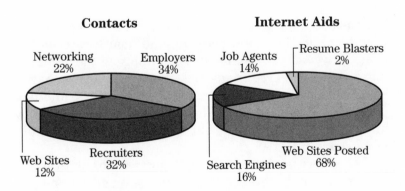

FIGURE 2.3: Contacts and Internet Aids by Type

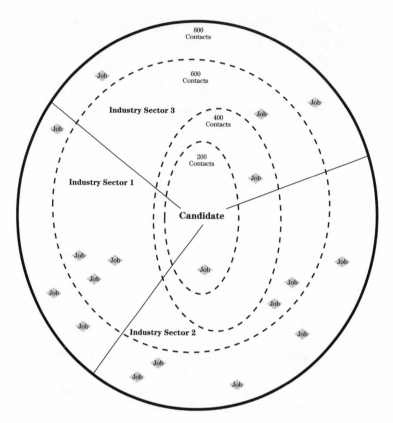

FIGURE 2.4: Casting the Net

health-care experience on your resume. Of course you would look in the manufacturing and health-care industries. However, your skills also can apply to the accounting and e-commerce industries, though you may never have worked in those industries. Herein lies another principle—your past gives you clues about where to start in your present situation, but it does not have to determine your future.

This perspective opens up all sorts of possibilities. It also makes it necessary to develop several versions of your resume, each focusing on industry-specific experience and using the correct jargon for that industry. Yes, it means more work. Beginning to get the idea?

CLARIFYING YOUR MOTIVATION

Motivation is an internal thing. We talk about people who are motivating, environments that are motivating, and other things that really motivate us. The truth is, motivation is a choice we make. No one can motivate us. We motivate ourselves.

Motivation is an energy that comes out of what you need. Your behavior in searching for a new executive position is motivated only by your needs and no one else's. You cannot directly motivate other people. They must motivate themselves. You must motivate yourself.

When we describe something as motivating us, what we are describing is the manner in which the person or the information touched our need and unlocked the door to our understanding how that need can be met. When that understanding leads to action, we have made a decision at some level to act. Only you can decide if this is going to work for you. Make up your mind right now that you have what it takes and you are going to patiently and diligently put into action what you will learn in this book.

You may believe you already know enough to carry out your search plan successfully. You're probably tempted to take shortcuts and dive right into some of the practical steps outlined in this book. Most of the executives I work with, eager to find a job and impatient with the process, take this tack at first, convinced they know themselves well enough to be able to identify what they need and don't need in terms of information or help.

Don't shortchange yourself. Take the time to work through the self-assessments provided. You will discover growth since the last time you took stock of what motivates you. Spend the time that's needed in order to plan effectively and use the organized approach we suggest for keeping track of your progress. Take stock of your emotions and let them inform you rather than manage you. Spend whatever time is necessary to become technologically informed about the Internet tools and techniques you will be introduced to. Think through strategies for communicating with recruiters and employers based on what you learn about how they think and how they work. Don't assume your savvy and charm will be enough.

Directing Your Motivation

1. Decide you are committed to the process and the work required.
2. Identify your ideal job, which capitalizes on who you are and what you need.
3. Learn yourself and your audience so well that the process of your candidacy flows like a river— it is inevitable that it will reach its destination.

Executives I work with are brilliant, at the top of their profession, real pros. They have no trouble with item number one, but almost to a person, they come to grips with numbers two and three only after taking shortcuts that didn't work.

UNDERSTANDING SUCCESS

Once you are committed to the process, you will find new freedom to adapt the steps to your own circumstance, reflecting your unique skills, experience, needs, and personality. Commitment is the key concept. You will not find that executive position with halfhearted efforts. Success comes with intelligent hard work.

And success is defined differently for different people and situations. There is no single magic formula.

Here are eight general comments and quotes about success. Each captures a different characteristic that applies to your search efforts.

1. The focus on doing what is right.

   "First say to yourself what you would be, then do what you have to do."

   —EPICTETUS

2. Character: The combination of qualities that determines a person's moral or ethical strength.

   "The most important thing for a young man is to establish a credit—a reputation, character."

   —JOHN D. ROCKEFELLER

3. Determination: Firmness or purpose toward a fixed intention.

   "Success seems to be largely a matter of hanging on after others have let go."

   —WILLIAM FEATHER

4. Enthusiasm: Great excitement or passion for a project, cause, or endeavor.

   "Nothing great was achieved without enthusiasm."

   —RALPH WALDO EMERSON

5. Initiative: The ability to begin a plan or task and follow it through energetically with enterprise and determination.

   "Initiative is to success what a lighted match is to a candle."

   —ORLANDO A. BATISTA

6. Integrity: Having steadfast adherence to a strict ethical or moral code.

   "Integrity without knowledge is weak and useless, and knowledge without integrity is dangerous and dreadful."

   —SAMUEL JOHNSON

7. Patience: The quality of being able to bear enduring difficulty, provocation, or annoyance with a
calm tolerance.

*"Let your patience show itself perfectly in what
you do. Then you will be perfect and complete and
will have everything you need."*

—THE APOSTLE JAMES

8. Preparation: The state of having been made
ready beforehand in anticipation of potential
obstacles.

*"It is thrifty to prepare today for the wants of to-
morrow."*

—AESOP

In the end, success will be what you define it to be,
and the measure of success in your search will not be the
position you land but the nature of the journey you
took getting there and whether or not you felt you had to
settle for less along the way.

CHAPTER 3

A LONG LOOK IN
THE MIRROR

A sense of satisfaction and challenge in the job helps to keep us motivated. Sure, happiness is a choice. It is also a feeling arising out of subliminal factors that are different for each of us. If you have been unhappy for an enduring amount of time it is worth the effort to sit down and figure out just what it is that is bugging you. Separate work issues from nonwork issues. Ask yourself some honest questions about the work issues.

- Am I having a personality conflict with someone?
- Do I like my coworkers?
- Do I get along with my leadership?
- Is the work I do enjoyable?
- Are the hours too long or scheduled poorly for my lifestyle?
- Is my contribution acknowledged?

- Do I know where my work fits into the grand scheme of things?
- Do I have a sense of being listened to, understood, and taken seriously?
- Do I envy others' compensation or feel bitter or resentful about my own?
- Do I live with the constant fear that I may be replaced?
- Are my expectations realistic under the circumstances?
- What are my goals, and are they being blocked?

The highly compensated and relatively secure executive doesn't spend much time considering these questions or the further questions the answers may produce. They seem just to be happy to be unhappy if that is the circumstance they find themselves in. Whether you need to find another job because you are dissatisfied with your present employment or because the one you have is going away—or worse, has gone away—this is a perfect opportunity to take stock. If you could design the perfect executive role, what would it look like?

WHO ARE YOU?

Assessing your current strengths, contributions, and goals is key to answering this question relative to your future career. Each of us reflects in the work we do an accumulation of experience, training, education, background, skills, talents, gifts, temperament, and personality. Though many times circumstances will require us to step outside our preferences for a period of time, there is a groove we each seem to work best in. Our groove also is where we find the most enjoyment in our work because what we do seems to flow naturally.

Another way to say this is that each of us has been designed to function best in certain environments, with certain tasks, and in certain relationships to our work and those we work with. When this happens, we call it a good job fit. Your design, in this sense, is constantly changing and maturing as you progress through various experiences in your life and career. What is important is understanding your *current* design and what that tells you about a good job fit, about the role that is just right for you, which should be an important consideration in your job search. No one intentionally becomes a square peg in a round hole.

Those who do not understand their design often lack a sense of purpose, may experience frequent boredom in the job, and experience continuing frustration. From a career perspective, this can be reflected in frequent job changes, confusion about career direction, and conflict at work. Burnout can occur if we are repeatedly required to perform tasks we don't like or are ill equipped to do or that leave our best skills unused, underused, or misused.

Understanding your design and factoring that knowledge into your job search will produce certain results. There is a sense of purpose and significance gained from work you enjoy doing. There is a sense of pacing and understanding that allows a greater degree of control and minimizes the frustration that a poor job fit causes. When the majority of your skills are used to accomplish tasks, when you're in a job that fits your design, your confidence and assurance are enhanced, giving you a stronger sense of direction. Self-assessment is the tool that enables you to choose job opportunities that make the best use of your design.

The goal is not a stress-free job. In fact, most people operate best under a certain amount of stress. But when you operate for too long outside the framework of your design you will become demotivated. And that's when job burnout and apathy on the job raise their ugly heads.

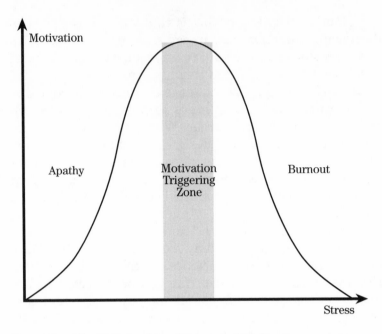

FIGURE 3.1: The Relationship of Stress and Motivation

Apathy is the result of too little of the right kind of stress. Burnout is the result of too much of the wrong kind of stress (see figure 3.1).

Exercise 1

Take a moment to jot down some reflections on your career history.

1. What were the situations in which you found yourself apathetic about a job? burned out on your job?

2. What were the specific factors that led to these feelings? Was it a working relationship, long hours, a terrible commute contributing to fatigue, something in

your personal life, the tasks you were required to perform, the culture where you worked, the leadership you were provided?

3. Try to identify what characterized the situation and what stimuli you were responding to. Make a list. These will be things to avoid in your next job.

A recently displaced manufacturing executive remembers a situation in which he became very apathetic about his job. His experience was being underutilized, and the CEO was a micromanager. The job became mundane and routine, unexciting. Another executive, in the transportation industry, worked for a micromanager as well. In his case, the boss (founder and chairman of the board) was a real driver, demanding unreasonable rework, long hours, and unreasonable deadlines. This executive got burned out. Apathy and burnout are predictable casualties for the committed executive.

From their reflections they both learned that, for very different reasons, they need jobs that provide a certain level of independence and don't involve someone looking over their shoulder all the time. Neither one of them enjoys cookie-cutter jobs where innovation and creativity have no reward. Jobs that require a consistent methodology, repetitive tasks, and a lot of structure are excellent motivating environments for a lot of people, but the highly compensated executive usually expects to and is expected to show initiative and operate independently.

Exercise 2

I asked both executives to think through all of their jobs from the most recent to the earliest and make a list of tasks, projects, and people they really enjoyed. Then I had them go through the list item by item and indicate on a table like the one in figure 3.2 what characteristic made that task, project, or person so enjoyable.

Both had numerous check marks for each characteristic. However, there were more check marks in some boxes than others. This makes sense, since each of these characteristics is used in varying degrees in every job. The characteristics that had more check marks provided clues regarding what role each would find the most satisfying. Now it is your turn.

Look at figure 3.2 and take a moment to check off the characteristics you most identify with. Have you had the most success in roles that grow organizations based on solid foundations (Building with a slight emphasis on Maintaining), or have you had the most success in roles that grow organizations based on new creative efforts (Building with an emphasis on Innovative)? All four of these characteristics will combine in different ways (not just the two illustrated), reflecting what you enjoy most, and will be consistent with the results of Exercise 1 in terms of what you do not enjoy.

Now you are equipped to ask the right questions when it comes time to research a company and prepare for an interview.

1. Just what kind of job is this?
2. Will it capitalize on what I enjoy most in a working environment?
3. Will it provide a climate that will interest and energize me?
4. Will it make good use of my most natural preferences?

A preference is a natural bent, habit, or pattern your work behavior reveals. It is a function of the skills you are most comfortable using, the social environments you feel most confident in, and the activities you find most rewarding personally.

Characteristic	Description	Occurrence
Practical	People are frank, persistent, and practical. Jobs produce specific results. Used mechanical abilities or analytical skills. Casual work environment.	
Maintaining	People are conscientious, orderly, systematic, and careful. Jobs are organized, follow procedures, and use scheduling. Used efficiency, analysis, and computational ability. Traditional work environment in both dress and work schedules.	
Building	People are competitive, aggressive, sociable, and adventuresome. Jobs involve people, leading, managing, or selling. Used interpersonal skills, verbal skills, and leadership skills. Flexible work environment requiring independent action.	
Innovative	People are friendly, understanding, ethical, and responsible. Jobs are open-ended, involve others, and provide recognition. Used listening skills, problem solving, and imagination. Changing work environment, variety, and multiple methods of formal and informal communication.	

FIGURE 3.2: Enjoyable Work Environment Characteristics

SIGNING BONUS:
INDUSTRY GROWTH AND
DECLINE ARE OPPORTUNITIES

Where should you look for this ideal role? A place to start is in industry sectors that are growing rapidly. A search of the top 25 career fields that are growing the fastest, have the most openings, and will constitute the largest occupational fields by the year 2008 reveals a rapidly changing landscape for the executive over the next decade (see figure 3.3).

These are just the top seven career fields. There are a growing number of opportunities to consider now and in the future. A result of growth in one industry is to increase vacancies in other industries as the workforce shifts in response to the labor shortage. In fact, 90 percent of the workforce will change jobs in the next seven years for a variety of reasons (see figure 3.4).

Not all of this is because of a better opportunity luring executives into expanding industries. Thirty percent of the companies that exist today will be off

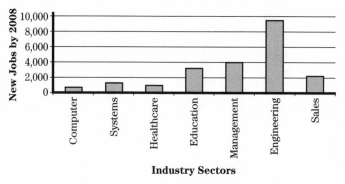

FIGURE 3.3: Fastest-Growing Career Fields

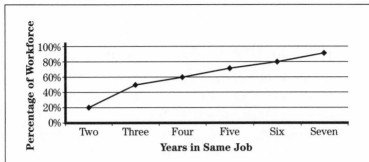

FIGURE 3.4: Job Change Frequency

the map, vanished, by the time we get to 2008. Mergers, acquisitions, downsizing, bankruptcy—there are all sorts of reasons. Even in these situations there is a need for skilled, experienced executives.

If you think this job search may be your last, take a look at the following list. It represents the 35-year job-change track record for a six-figure executive beginning with the first job after graduation from college.

First Job: Found a job in another state using the newspaper from a chosen city

Second Job: Recruited away to a different industry by the CEO of a new company

Third Job: Went into business with two partners

Fourth Job: Recruited away by a client to set up a similar business model in a different industry

Fifth Job: Recruited away by a client to set up a similar business in yet another industry

(continues)

INDUSTRY GROWTH AND DECLINE
ARE OPPORTUNITIES *(continued)*

Sixth Job: Recruited away to help a dying enterprise get back on its feet (this was the fourth change in industry)

Seventh Job: Left job number six when the handwriting was on the wall and found a turnaround job in the same industry career started in

Eighth Job: Left job seven when the turnaround was complete and searched for another executive position in a different industry

This executive has had eight jobs in 35 years, changing jobs approximately every four and a half years and working in five different industries. His experience is no different than 60 percent of all the executives out there.

Exercise 3

To build a functional understanding of your preferred skill set, it is necessary that you answer a few basic questions related to the most rewarding achievements of each employment experience you have had in your career. Answering these questions will help you identify the skill sets that are strengths for you.

Make a list of your most rewarding achievements, then answer the following questions about each one. The terms under Descriptions in figure 3.5 are designed to help you accurately describe your experience of the achievement. You may think of other terms as well. These are here just to stimulate your thinking. As you answer

Characteristic	Description	Terms
People	What kinds of people did I prefer to work with or serve? Men, women, children, people of a different cultural or social background, peers, subordinates, superiors, self-starters, those needing direction? What kinds of problems did I like to try to help people with? Work related, personal, analytical, relational, technical, process related, task related? In what environment did I like to work with people? Consultative, directive, individual, group, organizational?	
Things	What type of things did I prefer? Tools, high-tech, information, machinery, computer, procedures, policies, other? What did I prefer to do with things? Build, teach, word process, operate?	
Data	What type of data did I prefer to work with? Computer, manuals, facts, accounting? How was that data used? To analyze, synthesize, summarize, report, evaluate, implement?	
Ideas	What knowledge base is the information or the ideas representative of? Experience, research, consultation with others, performance history? How were the ideas presented? Written reports, presentations? Who was affected by the ideas? Individuals, groups, the company, processes, programs, procedures, revenue, costs?	

FIGURE 3.5: Enjoyable Work Environment Themes

the questions, note the terms that recur and make a separate list of them. This list represents what motivates you the most.

1. What was involved in the achievement? Describe it in detail.
2. What was your part?
3. What did you actually do?
4. How did you go about that?

Exercise 4

Now turn that list of terms into a list of specific skills. Refer back to your earlier work in this chapter for ideas. Go back and forth until you feel you have identified the skill set you enjoy using the most.

Using figure 3.6, list as many terms as necessary and identify as many skills as possible. Keep in mind this is descriptive of what you enjoy doing, not what you have to do or what you believe others expect you to do.

Exercise 5

Your preferences are reflected in how you use these skills. Exercise 5, "How Would You Describe Yourself?" (figure

Terms	Skills Used

FIGURE 3.6

3.8), will help identify the environment you naturally prefer to use these skills in. When you mark Risk, Focus, Pace, and Style, place an X somewhere in the range. For example, if you tend to be slightly more risk taking than cautious, your response may look like figure 3.7.

The object is not to be precise, just to identify generally how you perceive yourself in a work environment. It would be a great idea to ask someone who knows you to score you separately, then compare his or her evaluation with yours. If their perspective is very different from

FIGURE 3.7

How Would You Describe Yourself?

This assessment uses your visual intuitive response. Please place a mark in the range where it is most descriptive of your Risk, Focus, Pace, and Style in a work environment.

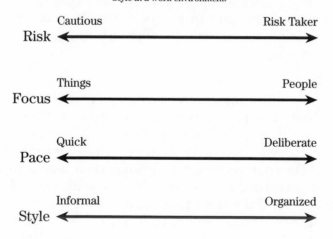

FIGURE 3.8

yours, have several people do the same thing and look for a consensus. Sometimes how we perceive ourselves is not how other people experience us.

Exercise 6

Now you are ready to create a few sentences describing your best contribution based on preferences. Here are a couple of examples:

• The transportation executive describes his best contribution this way: "I enjoy contributing most to new business growth requiring innovation in an environment of flexibility and independent responsibilities. I am a risk-taking people-person who enjoys a fast-paced, informal culture in which my interpersonal skills, imagination, and ability to communicate new ideas effectively is recognized and appreciated."

• The manufacturing executive describes his best contribution this way: "Building the business based on solid analysis and proven techniques has always given me the most success and the most enjoyable challenges. I prefer to work independently within relatively clear guidelines using my interpersonal skills, proven selling skills, and a systematic approach in a casual work environment.

Both executives have a good feel for what the next job opportunity may present by way of job fit. They are prepared to evaluate their design against the job requirements specifically stated and intuitively reinforced in each conversation they have with those who interview them. They can represent accurately their ability to contribute and what's more, they have specific examples to share when those questions get asked in the interview. They are also better equipped to avoid taking the wrong job, one that looked great on paper but just didn't pan out quite the way they expected because of all the unasked questions and unknown realities a job description never addresses.

Now it's your turn. Use figure 3.9 to create a few sentences describing your contribution.

Exercise 7

Once your contribution zone has been identified, it is helpful to identify the strengths that support this contribution and make it possible. This is an iterative process synthesizing the information you have developed already. Review your contribution statement several times. Your contribution statement may include several sentences as in the examples. In figure 3.10, list each of these sentences as a separate contribution. Change your strength list until you think you have captured what it

FIGURE 3.9: Contribution Statement

Contribution

Strengths

1.

2.

3.

4.

5.

6.

FIGURE 3.10

is that enables this contribution. Review the other material developed thus far for ideas you may have left out.

Exercise 8

Goals fall into two categories: What you want to achieve in your next career position and what you want to add to your inventory of strengths that will expand your contribution.

Finish this sentence: "I want a job that . . ." Turn it into one or more goal statements and include specifics like compensation and geography.

The manufacturing executive said, "My goal is to secure a position in executive sales management as vice president or chief operations officer with a high-tech or medical equipment manufacturer determined to grow their business nationally."

"My goal is to fill a role that reports to top executives, operates independently with accountability for results, and operates within mutually agreed upon targets with a defined timeline."

"My goal is to be rewarded with a market-rate base salary, sales budget–based bonus system of up to 30 percent of base, and standard benefits package for performance capitalizing on my ability to build winning sales teams and execute solid strategic sales planning."

He also had a few goals related to his continued development. An employer may or may not provide the opportunity for this to happen but it is something to consider when asking in detail what the job provides in terms of career growth or progression within the company.

"My goal is to develop expertise with the latest e-learning technology as it relates to manufacturing technology."

"My goal is to grow in my ability to step outside of traditional approaches to market analysis for healthcare forecasting in light of the increasing globalization of the market."

"My goal is to create and maintain my lifelong network so that I don't have to go through this job search process in quite the same painful way again!"

Though these goals obviously have a personal bias to them, they are all focused on the executive's career potential.

Figuring out how you are best designed to function and which industries and jobs can make the best use of that design in an enjoyable climate is not rocket science.

Actually, the process is simple—but it's not easy. All the information is there already. That's the easy part. The difficult part is committing to the process and disciplining yourself to do the work that matters. The beauty is that you only have to do this once.

From now on every career or job decision will be considered within the framework of who you now know yourself to be. Step back far enough to see the whole picture, remembering to validate that perception with others who know you.

Your Unique Selling Proposition (USP)

This product term became popular some years ago and holds a key concept for you to understand. If you were a brand-new automobile (instead of a highly paid, fire-eating executive) being introduced to the market, what would be the single most important set of reasons you could give consumers to persuade them to buy you over the competition? There are more than 8 million executives in this country earning six-figure incomes. What sets you apart from the herd?

Your USP is a unique description that sets you apart and will be reflected in the opening statements of your cover letter as well as your qualifications statement in your resume. This really is a focus statement that captures your contribution in appealing language that compels the readers to picture you leading them to greater success.

Your USP is about you and, more important, about your customers and what they are looking for. This is where you put on your customer-focus hat and picture yourself on the receiving end of a telephone call, resume, or interview. The USP describes what you can deliver. Generalizations will not help you. This is about results they can expect. Not everyone will respond to your succinctly worded description, nor would you want them to.

You are targeting an elite market with your USP and not the market at large. Here is how you do it:

1. Write out what it is you can do for the employer and how you will carry it out. Your contribution statement with associated strengths will supply the ideas you need to draft your first attempt at developing a USP.

2. Talk to a few colleagues who know you well and ask them if it resonates as true to them and if it's compelling. Emphasize that you're looking for honest feedback.

3. Carefully evaluate your draft.

- Does your draft USP target the opportunity or industry specifically enough?
- Does your USP combine contribution with results?
- Is your USP simple enough to memorize and reel off your tongue easily in conversation, or does it sound contrived?

4. Rewrite your USP.

5. Read your revised USP and jot down the value-added components that come to mind. If you were hiring this person, is this what you would be looking for?

6. Now boil it down to a single short paragraph. Remove any obscure or fuzzy statements until it is clear and distinct. Don't try to tighten things up on the first try—it will take several revisions to clean it up.

Here is an example: "I am a proven executive with extensive experience in medical device manufacturing operations in more than 60 countries. Known for capitalizing on growth and change and doubling profits in record time, success has been acknowledged through the National Association of Manufacturers award for business excellence—producing measurable improvements in supply change management, manufacturing processes, and global margins that drive the competition out of the market."

SIGNING BONUS:
WHY THINK OF YOURSELF AS UNEMPLOYED?

Consulting and contract work provide excellent opportunities to network, be introduced to potential employers, and provide additional income while you are searching. This is what I did some time ago when the last recession bumped me out of a job.

I was a senior vice president with a corporation that all but disappeared in the slowing economy. The terms of my severance agreement did not forbid my seeking consulting or contract work nor were they diminished at all by any income I earned during the period covered by the severance agreement. Severance agreements differ widely—your severance agreement may specify that salary and benefits continuation will be reduced by the amount of income you receive.

During my job search, I received and turned down three offers that simply did not live up to my requirements. Because I had a good idea of what constituted my ideal role I had the freedom to say no. Because I had an additional source of income I was not circumstantially required to settle for less. In the end, I took a job that fit my requirements almost one year after I had been laid off. Here is what I did.

1. I got on the Internet and learned what I needed to do to set up a sole proprietorship in the town I lived in. The city had a Web site with all the information I needed about a business license, a permit, and other documentary requirements.

2. With a few hundred dollars and a little legwork, I had a business and a bank account to handle the revenue, expenses, and tax obligations.

3. I obtained a federal employer identification number (EIN) over the telephone at no charge. Some employers will require this even if you have a business license and registered business name. And yes, I found the telephone number on the Internet.

4. My Internet service provider (ISP) included a free Web card (a one-page Web site) with my e-mail account, which I designed for the business and used as a marketing tool. I also took the trouble to purchase the domain name related to my business name.

5. Paper stock suitable for business cards was available at the local office supply store. Most business card stock sold in this manner comes with instructions for setting up standard word processing software to print the cards. I printed my own business cards. You may not have the equipment and software needed to do a professional job of this. No problem, it is not a large expense to have your own printed by a local print shop.

6. I created standard letterhead using my word processing software and printed it on an as-needed basis on professional stationery.

7. I joined a number of professional organizations and began attending meetings. I used my network to look for consulting and contracting opportunities as well as job leads. Every employer I interviewed was a potential client for consulting or contracting.

8. Using the Internet, I found and modified a boilerplate consulting agreement. I made sure it included an indemnification clause and, if appropriate and required, charged the client for insurance costs. A sole proprietorship does not offer the same

(continues)

WHY THINK OF YOURSELF AS UNEMPLOYED?

(continued)

protection of personal assets that a corporation does.

9. I registered with a number of consulting/ contracting Web sites on the Internet.

10. I interviewed with and was accepted into the fold of consulting organizations that use free-lancers. I found these on the Internet as well.

11. I contacted employers in the news because of their growth, downsizing, mergers, or acquisitions in case they had transitional situations I could use my USP to sell into.

12. What to charge was easy to figure out. There are many formulas to use in pricing consulting or contract jobs. However, I took a very simple approach. The rule of thumb is to work half of your available hours. The rest of the time is spent selling your services or looking for an executive position. There are 2,080 available work hours in a year. Half of this is 1,040. Consultants who work this much generally are pretty happy. Next, I divided my target annual income by 1,040 to get an hourly rate, added 20 percent for benefits and 10 percent for overhead.

THE IDEAL OPPORTUNITY

In the foregoing exercises, you outlined in general terms your ideal opportunity. Now you need to add specific qualifiers.

- What compensation do you need?
- What would you like under the best of circumstances?

Let's say your target income is $160,000. With this approach you need to charge $200 per hour.

13. Now for a reality check. What is the going rate in your industry for consulting work? How does this figure compare with the rate you came up with? If your first estimate is too high, take out the overhead margin. This can be charged separately as a direct expense in your consulting agreement. Your benefits may be already covered by your severance agreement, making this customer expense unnecessary. Now your hourly rate is reduced to approximately $150 per hour. Target income can be adjusted as well. The goal is to arrive at a competitive rate that does not undersell your skills.

During my unemployment "employment," I had a number of clients for my executive coaching services and also found work with a number of varied organizations, including a leading benefits provider, a bank, a merger and acquisition consulting firm, a casino, an international nonprofit organization, and a medical center. The longest job lasted seven weeks, the shortest, a single day of training. The offer I finally did accept came from one of my clients.

You don't have to be unemployed while you are in a career transition.

- What is the bottom line—the deal breaker—for you?
- Can you relocate?
- Are there geographical limitations on where you can relocate?
- Can you work virtually (telecommute)?

Later we will discuss compensation specifics. Answering these questions is designed to estimate where you are willing to work and for how much. Now take a separate sheet of paper and title it "Ideal Job." Put your USP at the top of the page. List the industries you are interested in. Next review your exercise results for descriptions of the work environment best suited to your preferences. Finish with the compensation and geographic requirements. This information will be honed through the following chapters. For now, you have a good initial picture of the ideal job and the ideal job fit.

CHAPTER 4

MARKETING YOURSELF

Now comes one of the most important steps in the entire process: telling your story—marketing you. Having a good understanding of the career mentality and a clear view of what you are setting out to do (see chapter 2) is critical to this step. Knowing who you are and what you are passionate about (see chapter 3) provides the ammunition needed to clearly communicate who you are, what you've done, what you know, and, more important, what you can bring to a new employer.

WHAT IS THE PURPOSE OF YOUR RESUME?

I ask candidates this question every day, and almost no one knows the right answer. And the right answer is *to get an interview*. Think about this: Employers don't hire from resumes. Now, mind you, there are always exceptions, but this is the rule and it is rarely broken. So let's play percentages and develop a marketing piece that will get you in front of hiring managers—the people who have the ability to offer you a job.

Selling yourself is the same as selling anything else. You develop a list of prospects (high-level hiring managers in organizations where you would like to work), you prioritize them (in order to make the best use of your time), you get your marketing piece (resume) in front of them, and you follow up with a telephone call for the sole purpose of obtaining an interview—an opportunity to meet them face-to-face. In chapter 8, we discuss what to do after you get an interview, but right now we have to concentrate on getting the interview.

WHICH RESUME TYPE PRESENTS YOU BEST?

There are only three commonly used types of resumes: chronological, functional, and focused. And the resume of choice is the chronological. Let's look at these one at a time.

Chronological Resume

The *chronological resume* (figure 4.1) is a historical review of your background, usually beginning with your most recent experience and working backward. As stated earlier, most people don't look for new jobs often enough to get really good at the process, so it is typical to do what everyone else is doing and develop a chronological resume. Sometimes this is good, sometimes this is bad.

The chronological resume is a good choice when you have been in the same industry for many years and have a consistent track record of promotions. It works very well when a prospective employer can see a logical

John Job-Seeker
1234 Any Street
Any Town, USA 12345
123-456-7891
jjobseeker@jobseeker.com
http://www.jobseeker.com

SENIOR EXECUTIVE PROFILE
Revenue and profit driven executive successful in vision casting, discovering
opportunities, creating and building organizations, and delivering strong results.

AREAS OF EXPERTISE:
* Strategic & Tactical Planning
* Revenue & Profit Growth
* Sales & Marketing Leadership
* Business Planning & Forecasting
* Competitive Analysis & Positioning
* New Market & Customer Development
* Hiring, Training & Mentoring
* Team Development & Leadership

PROFESSIONAL EXPERIENCE
JJ Jones & Company   1997–Present
Fast-track promotions through a series of increasingly responsible senior
management positions for emerging ventures.

Vice President of Business Development & Sales (2001–Present)
Designed and implemented new global corporate vision and strategy and
positioned JJ Jones as a leader in Business Effectiveness Solutions.

Member of 6-person Senior Executive Committee commissioned by the CEO of
JJ Jones to translate strategy into action. Group was created to design and
recommend global strategy for new business growth initiatives.
> * Collaborated with committee to plan, design, and implement the
>   global business growth initiatives plan.
> * Credited with the successful and profitable start-up of JJ Jones
>   business growth initiatives plan. Appointed to Vice President of
>   Business Development & Sales.
> * Performed market needs analysis and developed segmentation
>   strategy, ensuring accurate positioning.
> * Designed and implemented sales training initiatives to train sales
>   teams on new products and services to existing clients.
> * Established and negotiated strategic productive business
>   partnerships with Customer Relationship Management (CRM)
>   providers to support business plan.

Vice President of Business Development and Marketing (1997–2001)
Accelerated profitable growth through establishment of new business unit and
servicing the manufacturing and aerospace industries.

Senior management responsibility for strategic and tactical planning of new
venture. Managed a team of 34. Reported directly to President.
> * Collaborated with Executive Committee to create market
>   analysis, product development, and strategy for newly established
>   group.
> * Planned, designed, and recommended strategic and operational
>   infrastructure, including staffing, technology, training, and
>   sales/marketing strategies.

(continues)

FIGURE 4.1: Chronological Resume

FIGURE 4.1: Chronological Resume, *continued*

* Designed and implemented a comprehensive sales training program to successfully penetrate manufacturing and aerospace markets. Successfully rolling out program to over 50 national sales executives.

Peterson Corporation   1988–1997
Promoted through a series of increasingly responsible sales and business development management positions for this company.

Director of New Business Development (1995–1997)
Established and penetrated marketplace through acquisition of client corporate communication solutions.

Senior management responsibility for strategic and tactical planning, sales and business development, and corporate culture of new business unit. Managed a sales team of 15. Reported directly to President.
* Designed and implemented new business development strategy achieving $35M in annual sales within 16 months.
* Hired, trained, and mentored sales professionals to successfully manage Peterson's largest account.
* Established and managed onsite sales campus to support customer's needs, including hiring/training, processes and procedures, organizational and customer service strategies.
* Introduced and educated customer on Peterson's new business solutions, resulting in more than $6M in yearly incremental revenue growth in 1995.
* Educated more than 300 outside Sales Executives on sales strategy and successfully introduced new products and services to existing customers.
* Collaborated with plant manager to integrate and educate more than 200 plant employees on Peterson's vision and culture resulting in improved gross profits of 47% within 8 months.

Regional Sales Manager (1988–1995)
Accelerated market growth of business communication solutions throughout the Northeastern United States.

Responsible for strategic and business development, sales and account management
* Formalized and managed strategic territory marketing plans, successfully increasing sales by 49% within $2^{1}/_{2}$ years.
* Developed, implemented, and directed all management initiatives, valued at over $15M in yearly sales.
* Redesigned new process for producing and distributing communication solutions, resulting in increasing revenue by $15M and achieving recognition as Businessman of the Year in 1995 in Any Town, USA.

EDUCATION/PROFESSIONAL TRAINING
* Quality Regional College, Bachelor of Arts Degree
* Well-Known Business School, MBA
* World-Renowned University, Special Business Solutions Program

Keywords: Vice President of Business Development, Vice President of Marketing, Vice President of New Business Opportunities

progression from one position to the next within the same field or closely related fields without any breaks in experience. It doesn't work so well when you are trying to change careers, when your work record has holes in it, or when you are concerned about your age.

Functional Resume

A *functional (skill-based) resume* (figure 4.2) often may be a better choice. A functional resume is based on your experience. It requires a different and slightly more challenging organization because you organize your experience by the functions you are most competent in. I don't see this type of resume often because most people are not aware of how it can be used effectively.

The functional resume is a good choice when you are planning on changing careers because it gives you an opportunity to communicate about your transferable skills. For example, you may be in the world of education right now, be gifted in analytical skills, and want to go into business. You have used these skills consistently, deliberately, and effectively in your present work. Now you have an opportunity to take your effectiveness in your contribution to the education field and apply it to a business situation. I consistently remind job seekers that employers are hiring results. This is a terrific opportunity to demonstrate your results.

For job seekers who have a work record that shows many different positions in many different companies or industries, the functional resume provides an opportunity for finessing the record. This does not mean lying. You must never lie on a resume or on any other application materials because, aside from the moral question, this can become immediate grounds for dismissal. What we are talking about here is to emphasize your accomplishments in various skill categories and to deemphasize areas where you are not as strong. For example, if you have moved from one industry to another or had positions that appear to be unrelated, it might be advisable to use a functional resume so that you can draw out the great experiences you have had, explain your accomplishments, and demonstrate the benefits gained from cross-training in different industries. This might very well raise you above the competition because you bring a totally fresh and enriched viewpoint to the job. Many companies today are looking for this breadth of experience.

Older workers can also benefit from this approach. Age discrimination is illegal in the United States, but it still happens. Many older workers in the six-figure category are being laid off or retired as businesses continue the process of driving profits to the bottom line. Many of these people cannot afford to retire, and many of those who can, don't want to. If you have years of experience, your chronological resume could go on for many pages. This is not a good idea. If you truncate your experience, for example, showing only the last 20 years, you must be very careful to be consistent so that you don't leave "age clues" in your resume. Remember: The goal is to get an interview.

Once in an interview, your age is apparent, but it does not have to be a problem because you will be prepared to demonstrate your competence and accomplishments. And the process of preparing a functional resume will help you do this effectively.

Focused Resume

The *focused resume* (figure 4.3) is a kind of hybrid of the functional and the chronological. It is especially effective when you are applying for a specific position and you can research the company and the requirements of the position.

In this case, you want to tailor as much of your experience as possible to the specifics of the position and

John Job-Seeker
1234 Any Street
Any Town, USA 12345
123-456-7891
jjobseeker@jobseeker.com
http://www.jobseeker.com

SENIOR EXECUTIVE PROFILE
Revenue and profit driven executive successful in vision casting, discovering opportunities, creating and building organizations, and delivering strong results.

AREAS OF EXPERTISE:
* Strategic & Tactical Planning
* Revenue & Profit Growth
* Sales & Marketing Leadership
* Business Planning & Forecasting
* New Market & Customer Development
* Hiring, Training & Mentoring
* Team Development & Leadership

CAPABILITIES

Strategic & Tactical Planning
> * Member of 6-person senior executive committee commissioned by the CEO to translate strategy into action. Group was created to design and recommend global strategy for new business growth initiatives.
> * Performed market needs analysis and developed segmentation strategy, ensuring accurate positioning.
> * Established and negotiated strategic productive business partnerships with customer relationship management (CRM) providers to support business plan.
> * Planned, designed, and recommended strategic and operational infrastructure, including staffing, technology, training, and sales/marketing strategies.
> * Senior management responsibility for strategic and tactical planning, sales and business development and corporate culture of new business unit. Managed a sales team of 15. Reported directly to President.

Revenue & Profit Growth
> * Credited with the successful and profitable start-up of business growth initiatives plan. Appointed to Vice President of Business Development & Sales.
> * Accelerated profitable growth through establishment of new business unit and servicing the manufacturing and aerospace industries.
> * Redesigned new process for producing and distributing communication solutions, resulting in increasing revenue by $15M and achieving recognition as Businessman of the Year in 1995 in Any Town, USA.

Sales & Marketing Leadership
> * Designed and implemented new business development strategy achieving $35M in annual sales within 16 months.
> * Formalized and managed strategic territory marketing plans, successfully increasing sales by 49% within $2^{1}/_{2}$ years.

Business Planning & Forecasting
> * Collaborated with committee to plan, design, and implement the global business growth initiatives plan.

(continues)

FIGURE 4.2: Functional Resume

FIGURE 4.2: Functional Resume, *continued*

* Designed and implemented new global corporate vision and strategy and positioned company as a leader in business effectiveness solutions.

Competitive Analysis & Positioning
* Developed, implemented, and directed all management initiatives, valued at over $15M in yearly sales.
* Collaborated with executive committee to create market analysis, product development, and strategy for newly established group.

New Market & Customer Development
* Senior management responsibility for strategic and tactical planning of new venture. Managed a team of 34. Reported directly to President.
* Established and managed onsite sales campus to support customer's needs, including hiring/training, processes and procedures, organizational and customer service strategies.
* Introduced and educated customer on Peterson's new business solutions, resulting in more than $6M in yearly incremental revenue growth in 1995.
* Collaborated with plant manager to integrate and educate more than 200 plant employees on Peterson's vision and culture resulting in improved gross profits of 47% within 8 months.

Hiring, Training & Mentoring
* Designed and implemented sales training initiatives to train sales teams on new products and services to existing clients.
* Designed and implemented a comprehensive sales training program to successfully penetrate manufacturing and aerospace markets. Successfully rolling out program to over 50 national sales executives.
* Hired, trained, and mentored sales professionals to successfully manage Peterson's largest account.
* Educated more than 300 outside Sales Executives on sales strategy and successfully introduced new products and services to existing customers.

PROFESSIONAL EXPERIENCE
JJ Jones & Company   1999–Present
Vice President of Business Development & Sales (2000–Present)
Fast-track promotions through a series of increasingly responsible senior management positions for emerging ventures.

Peterson Corporation   1991–1999
Director of New Business Development (1997–1999)
Promoted through a series of increasingly responsible sales and business development management positions for this company.

EDUCATION/PROFESSIONAL TRAINING
* Quality Regional College, Bachelor of Arts Degree
* Well-Known Business School, MBA
* World-Renowned University, Special Business Solutions Program

Keywords: Vice President of Business Development, Vice President of Marketing, Vice President of New Business Opportunities

the company, showing how your skills, training, and experience might contribute effectively to your targeted company. Hiring managers are busy people and don't always have the time to figure out how you might fit in their organizations. The more you can do to market yourself through your resume, the greater your chance of being invited for an interview. And, after all, that's the only purpose for a resume.

Three other resume types are used in some cases: qualifications brief, functions-features-accomplishments-benefits profile, and the verbal resume.

Qualifications Brief

The *qualifications brief* is a prose summary of your work experience. Often, consultants use this to summarize their work experience and highlight their strengths and focus areas. It is not an effective means to communicate with prospective employers and is not recommended for this purpose.

Functions-Features-Accomplishments-Benefits Resume

On the other hand, the *functions-features-accomplishments-benefits resume* (figure 4.4) is a very effective way to communicate with hiring managers, although it is not often used. However, it is valuable because it clearly and effectively communicates your accomplishments and how they can be applied to new experiences. Remember, hiring managers are hiring results.

This is a fairly typical approach in sales and, after all, that's what you are doing here—with yourself as your product. It's a very effective way to present your

John Job-Seeker
1234 Any Street
Any Town, USA 12345
123-456-7891
jjobseeker@jobseeker.com
http://www.jobseeker.com

SENIOR EXECUTIVE PROFILE
Revenue and profit driven executive successful in vision casting, discovering opportunities, creating and building organizations, and delivering strong results seeking a position as Vice President for Corporate Communications.

AREAS OF EXPERTISE:
* Strategic & Tactical Planning
* Revenue & Profit Growth
* Sales & Marketing Leadership
* Business Planning & Forecasting
* Competitive Analysis & Positioning
* New Market & Customer Development
* Hiring, Training & Mentoring
* Team Development & Leadership

PROFESSIONAL EXPERIENCE
JJ Jones & Company   1997–Present
Fast-track promotions through a series of increasingly responsible senior management positions for emerging ventures.

Vice President of Business Development & Sales (2001–Present)
Designed and implemented new global corporate vision and strategy and positioned JJ Jones as a leader in Business Effectiveness Solutions.

Member of 6-person Senior Executive Committee commissioned by the CEO of JJ Jones to translate strategy into action. Group was created to design and recommend global strategy for new business growth initiatives.
   * Collaborated with committee to plan, design, and implement the global business growth initiatives plan.
   * Credited with the successful and profitable start-up of JJ Jones business growth initiatives plan. Achieved increased profit of 17% over previous year. Appointed to Vice President of Business Development & Sales.
   * Performed market needs analysis and developed segmentation strategy, ensuring accurate positioning. Sales increase of 5%.
   * Designed and implemented sales training initiatives to train sales teams on new products and services to existing clients. Sales person retention rate doubled over two years.
   * Established and negotiated strategic productive business partnerships with Customer Relationship Management (CRM) providers to support business plan. Increased revenues by $650,000.

Vice President of Business Development and Marketing (1997–2001)
Accelerated profitable growth through establishment of new business unit and servicing the manufacturing and aerospace industries.

Senior management responsibility for strategic and tactical planning of new venture. Managed a team of 34. Reported directly to President.
   * Collaborated with Executive Committee to create market analysis, product development, and strategy for newly established group. Contributed additional 12% to bottom line.

FIGURE 4.3: Focused Resume

       * Planned, designed, and recommended strategic and operational
         infrastructure, including staffing, technology, training, and
         sales/marketing strategies.
       * Designed and implemented a comprehensive sales training program
         to successfully penetrate manufacturing and aerospace markets.
         Successfully rolling out program to over 50 national sales executives.

Peterson Corporation   1988–1997
Promoted through a series of increasingly responsible sales and business
development management positions for this company.

Director of New Business Development (1995–1997)
Established and penetrated marketplace through acquisition of client corporate
communication solutions.

Senior management responsibility for strategic and tactical planning, sales and
business development, and corporate culture of new business unit. Managed a
sales team of 15. Reported directly to President.
       * Designed and implemented new business development strategy
         achieving $35M in annual sales within 16 months.
       * Hired, trained, and mentored sales professionals to successfully
         manage Peterson's largest account. Increased sales by 11%.
       * Established and managed onsite sales campus to support
         customer's needs, including hiring/training, processes and
         procedures, organizational and customer service strategies.
       * Introduced and educated customer on Peterson's new business
         solutions, resulting in more than $6M in yearly incremental
         revenue growth in 1995.
       * Educated more than 300 outside Sales Executives on sales
         strategy and successfully introduced new products and services
         to existing customers.
       * Collaborated with plant manager to integrate and educate more
         than 200 plant employees on Peterson's vision and culture
         resulting in improved gross profits of 47% within 8 months.

Regional Sales Manager (1988–1995)
Accelerated market growth of business communication solutions throughout
the Northeastern United States.

Responsible for strategic and business development, sales and account
management
       * Formalized and managed strategic territory marketing plans,
         successfully increasing sales by 49% within 2$1/2$ years.
       * Developed, implemented, and directed all management initiatives,
         valued at over $15M in yearly sales.
       * Redesigned new process for producing and distributing
         communication solutions, resulting in increasing revenue by $15M
         and achieving recognition as Businessman of the Year in 1995 in
         Any Town, USA.

EDUCATION/PROFESSIONAL TRAINING
       * Quality Regional College, Bachelor of Arts Degree
       * Well-Known Business School, MBA
       * World-Renowned University, Special Business Solutions Program

Keywords: Vice President of Business Development, Vice President of
Marketing, President of New Business Opportunities

background and experience to an employer. More important, you show a prospective employer how your employment will benefit both the organization as a whole and the employer as an individual. The goal is to demonstrate how you can help improve profits, reduce costs, and just make things run better.

This type of resume includes four parts:

1. Functions: What you can do. Specifically detail all of the functional work you can do (coordinate a merger, close sales, manage a division, and so on).

2. Features: Who you are. List facts about yourself (strengths, interests, abilities).

3. Accomplishments: What you have done. Include significant measurable results you obtained for your current and past employers. These should either be quantifiable (concrete numbers, fractions, dollars, percentages) or qualifiable (carefully crafted descriptions of qualities achieved, improved morale, heightened esprit de corps, more robust planning sessions). It's important to note that quantifiable results carry more weight because they are easier to understand and document.

4. Benefits: How you can add value to a new employer. Make educated guesses about what you can do for a new employer based on your accomplishments.

Here's how you do this. Because of the work you did in chapter 3, this should be easy. Start by preparing a chronology of your work history. This is a draft so include everything—all of the positions you have held and the promotions and awards you've received. After preparing the chronological history, make a list of all of the functional work you have ever done. Next, list all of your strengths or features. This list might include analytical, decision maker, strategic planner, and so on. Then list all of your significant accomplishments for each position. It's important to list everything, and remember to quantify and qualify. If you can't do that, then there is a very real question whether the item should be included.

Finally, show specifically what you can do for the new employer. This is going to be based on what you know about the prospective employer: the business, the position, the economy, and the person you would report to. If you have a position description, understand it completely. Then, write your benefits section based upon what the company says it is looking for. The USP you developed in chapter 3 should be included here. This is where you show them how who you are fits what they are looking for.

Many job descriptions are not very well written. They often include examples of what an employer wants you to have (a BA degree, 10 years' experience) rather than what they want you to do (increase sales by 15 percent in the first year, increase profits at the bottom line by 5 percent in year one). Your challenge is to take whatever is dealt to you and turn it into an effective benefits presentation. Based on your best guess, what can the prospective employer expect to gain by hiring you?

Be thorough in this process. Review carefully. Ask people who know you well to review your work. Can they think of other things that should be included? Have you communicated clearly and concisely? Are there any other quantifiable or qualifiable results you can include? And be sure to consider your entire career. There may be some accomplishment from early in your work experience that is particularly appropriate for this presentation.

The final thing to do is to clean up the presentation. Remove the extraneous material. Format the document so it reads well and easily. And keep it to two pages or less. I am aware that many career consultants recommend keeping a resume to one page but of all the hundreds of resumes I see, no more than 5 percent are one page, and these are usually from people with little or no experience. I have never had an employer complain

John Job-Seeker
1234 Any Street
Any Town, USA 12345
123-456-7891
jjobseeker@jobseeker.com
http://www.jobseeker.com

SENIOR EXECUTIVE PROFILE
Revenue and profit driven executive successful in vision casting, discovering opportunities, creating and building organizations, and delivering strong results.

FUNCTIONS
* Established and negotiated strategic productive business partnerships
* Performed market needs analysis and developed segmentation strategy
* Redesigned new process for producing and distributing communication solutions
* Strategic and tactical planning
* Designed and implemented new business development strategy
* Designed the global business growth initiatives plan
* Market analysis, product development and strategy
* Introduced and educated customers on new business solutions
* Designed and implemented a comprehensive sales training program
* Hired, trained, and mentored sales professionals

FEATURES
* Analytical	* Hard-driving
* Strategist	* Good listener
* Visionary	* Salesman
* Organized	* Communicator
* Planner	* Teacher
* Self-disciplined	* Mentor
* Goal-oriented	

ACCOMPLISHMENTS
Strategic & Tactical Planning
* Member of 6-person senior executive committee commissioned by the CEO to translate strategy into action. Group was created to design and recommend global strategy for new business growth initiatives.
* Performed market needs analysis and developed segmentation strategy, ensuring accurate positioning.
* Established and negotiated strategic productive business partnerships with customer relationship management (CRM) providers to support business plan.
* Planned, designed, and recommended strategic and operational infrastructure, including staffing, technology, training, and sales/marketing strategies.
Revenue & Profit Growth
* Credited with the successful and profitable start-up of business growth initiatives plan. Appointed to Vice President of Business Development & Sales.
* Accelerated profitable growth through establishment of new business unit and servicing the manufacturing and aerospace industries.
* Redesigned new process for producing and distributing communication solutions, resulting in increasing revenue by $15M and achieving recognition as Businessman of the Year in 1995 in Any Town, USA.Sales & Marketing Leadership
* Designed and implemented new business development strategy achieving $35M in annual sales within 16 months.
* Formalized and managed strategic territory marketing plans, successfully increasing sales by 49% within $2^{1}/_{2}$ years.

FIGURE 4.4: Functions-Features-Accomplishments-Benefits Resume

Business Planning & Forecasting
* Collaborated with committee to plan, design and implement the global business growth initiatives plan.
* Designed and implemented new global corporate vision and strategy and positioned company as a leader in business effectiveness solutions.

Competitive Analysis & Positioning
* Developed, implemented and directed all management initiatives, valued at over $15M in yearly sales.
* Collaborated with executive committee to create market analysis, product development and strategy for newly established group.

New Market & Customer Development
* Senior management responsibility for strategic and tactical planning of new venture. Managed a team of 34. Reported directly to President.
* Established and managed onsite sales campus to support customer's needs, including hiring/training, processes and procedures, organizational and customer service strategies.
* Introduced and educated customers new business solutions, resulting in more than $6M in yearly incremental revenue growth in 1995.

Hiring, Training & Mentoring
* Designed and implemented sales training initiatives to train sales teams on new products and services to existing clients.
* Designed and implemented a comprehensive sales training program to successfully penetrate manufacturing and aerospace markets. Successfully rolling out program to over 50 national sales executives.
* Hired, trained and mentored sales professionals to successfully manage Peterson's largest account.

BENEFITS
* Strategic planning skills and experience allow me to create a future for my employer that will increase the company's effectiveness in reaching the target market thus increasing the bottom line.
* My experience in consistently increasing revenues and profits will benefit my new organization because I know how to bring in more sales while squeezing out more profits.
* Sales are increased by motivating and energizing the sales force to accomplish more by doing the right things at the right times as a team thus creating a more positive esprit de corps that results in a better bottom line.

PROFESSIONAL EXPERIENCE
JJ Jones & Company   1999–Present
Vice President of Business Development & Sales (2000–Present)
Fast-track promotions through a series of increasingly responsible senior management positions for emerging ventures.

Peterson Corporation   1991–1999
Director of New Business Development (1997–1999)
Promoted through a series of increasingly responsible sales and business development management positions for this company.

EDUCATION/PROFESSIONAL TRAINING
* Quality Regional College, Bachelor of Arts Degree
* Well-Known Business School, MBA
* World-Renowned University, Special Business Solutions Program

Keywords: Vice President of Business Development, Vice President of Marketing, Vice President of New Business Opportunities

about a two-page resume. It's not size that is the issue. It's the content!

Job seekers with sales experience will quickly see the advantages of this approach. Other professionals may think, "That's a lot of work." And, of course, they are correct. But this is what it takes to move to the next level. And, right now, this is the most important thing you are doing. When you've completed this document, you will know *you* better than ever before.

And when you have a strong presentation, you will find it much easier to look for that next position. If you don't have a good presentation, you won't prospect, you can't negotiate, and ultimately you won't be able "to close the sale." Memorize the content of this presentation—especially how you will benefit a company—and have it ready to use at a moment's notice.

When you go to your interviews, take your FFAB sheet with you. Be sure to answer questions by relying on your FFAB information—especially to emphasize how you can benefit the new company.

Verbal Resume

This material becomes the heart of the *verbal resume* (figure 4.5). This type of resume is used all the time and yet most people are unaware they are using it and so don't spend any time preparing it. How many times has someone asked you these questions?

What are you looking for?

What have you done?

What is the ideal situation for you?

If you could do anything you want, what would you do?

What drives you?

What are you passionate about?

What is your life's purpose?

What do you offer a company?

What can you do for me?

When you have completed and memorized your FFAB resume presentation you will have the answers for these and many more questions.

Work on developing a fifteen-second verbal presentation. I call this "the elevator speech." It's the amount of time you have to answer the question, "What do you do?" between the fifth and sixth floor on an elevator. You never know who you may meet on an elevator and if you provide an effective response to the question, you just might get an interview. The Boy Scout motto "Be Prepared" applies here in spades.

Hi, my name is John Job-Seeker.

I'm a results driven executive who has been successful in creating vision, finding opportunities, building organizations, and delivering strong revenues and profits.

And I've been able to do this in spite of the economy and intense competition.

Through my extensive experience conceiving and delivering comprehensive growth programs to my market area I have been instrumental in building successful sales departments that have consistently delivered more revenue to the bottom line.

As you can tell, I communicate easily, quickly gaining support from my team members. This makes it possible to work effectively and profitably to move my company forward.

I have done this for several companies in the past and I am confident I can do it again for another company that wants to gain market share and make more money.

FIGURE 4.5: Verbal Resume

WHAT FORM SHOULD YOU USE?

As stated above, the appearance of the resume is not nearly as important as the content. However, if the appearance does not draw the hiring manager in, the content won't matter.

My goal is to always make it easy for the hiring manager. They, like everyone else in today's world, are very busy. Remember, in most cases, they have full-time responsibilities without the added burden of hiring someone. Usually, this person has far more to get done than he or she has time to do. After all, that's why they are hiring someone. Now, he or she has the added burden of reviewing scores of resumes—many of which are from job seekers not remotely qualified for the position.

It's important to keep this point in mind. It may very well be the fault of the organization for attracting so many resumes from unqualified candidates. This happens because job descriptions are not well written and do not precisely spell out what the successful candidate must do to succeed. This provides a terrific opportunity for the successful job seeker to shine. Because you have prepared a functions-features-accomplishments-benefits resume you can demonstrate the value you can add to the organization.

You will need three forms of resumes to succeed in today's business world: 1) the formatted word processor document, 2) the text document (also referred to as an ASCII document), and 3) the Web-based resume. The content will probably be identical and only the form of presentation will change.

Formatted Word Processor Resume

The rich text formatted (RTF) word processor document is excellent for in-person presentations. This format transfers well from one word processor program to another. So if you are using Microsoft Word and someone else is using Corel WordPerfect the document will transfer intact. You should always carry several of these with you so you can hand them to someone after you have made a verbal presentation. And I would recommend it be done in that order. When you make a verbal presentation you want the listener to be listening, not reading. But, you also want to leave a "snapshot" of yourself. This is the purpose of the word processor resume.

It's extremely important to understand that in today's electronic world nearly all resumes go in one of two places: the wastebasket or the electronic database. And if you have not carefully prepared your resume it may not make much difference.

Text (ASCII) Resume

In order to get a resume into a database it has to be in a text format. If you hand deliver a hard copy or attach a word processor document to an e-mail, it has to be converted into text before it can be added to a database. If the person has a hard copy of the resume, it means the hard copy must be scanned, converted into text through an OCR utility, edited and corrected, then uploaded to that database. That's a lot of work, and remember our goal is to simplify the life of the hiring manager. If you've provided an attachment, it can be opened, saved as a text document, and uploaded. That's much easier and faster.

But, this can also be a problem. If that word processor resume is too beautiful, that is, has too much fancy formatting, it will not convert to text very well. I occasionally receive resumes that use extensive tables and elaborate formatting. When these are converted to text, they turn into garbled messes of largely unintelligible words and phrases.

So, here's how to handle this challenge. After you have completed your resume document save it in a word processing program with all the formatting in place. Then, save it again as a text document. Open it up and study it. Does is still make an excellent presentation? If not, work on it to make it look as attractive as a text document can look. Remember, you do not have normal, word processing formatting available in a text document, other than some font choices. You must get creative and use capitals and various keyboard symbols, such as !@#$%^&*()_ to draw attention to your sections and main points. I don't recommend getting fancy with fonts either because many database conversion processes only allow a limited and simple font selection. If you are a visual person this will probably be very frustrating to you, but remember: The goal is to communicate with the hiring manager.

Web-Based Resume

The Web-based resume is just one more tool in your job-search toolbox. There is considerable debate today around whether this form of resume will eventually become the form of choice or whether it will vanish from the scene. The answer is probably somewhere in between, and until that question has been resolved, it's worth having one online.

There is also some confusion about what to call this type of resume. Sometimes any electronic document is referred to as a Web-based resume. Therefore, a scannable resume might be referred to as a Web-based resume. For our purposes, a Web-based resume is one that is located on a server on the Internet that can be accessed on the World Wide Web. This resume may be nothing more than your standard resume uploaded to a site that accepts resumes, or it may be much more elaborate. If you are uploading your resume to a career or employment site, be cautious about using too much formatting. You will have to learn the rules for each site so that you can upload the appropriate form of resume—formatted, html, or text.

Many people are creating their own extensive re-sume Web site and either uploading it to a community such as Tripod or GeoCities or acquiring their own do-main name and address.

As with any new technology, there are pros and cons about its use. First the pros:

• Anybody who has an Internet connection can ac-cess your resume if they know the address or uniform re-source locator (URL). This increases your exposure, thus increasing your career opportunities.

• You can present far more information than in a typical text or word-processed document, including graphics, charts, and photographs. (See this address for an example of an elaborate resume site: www.chakkour .com.) There is no size limitation. Typically, you would include the same basic information that you have in-cluded on your word-processed or text document with links to additional information. This allows the viewer to determine what he or she wants to see.

• Your personal style can shine much better in this presentation.

The cons are:

• Anybody who has an Internet connection can access your resume if they know the URL (address). This can be a problem if you are presently employed and your employer finds your resume.

• You might give a prospective employer too much information and thus negate the opportunity of getting an interview.

Who uses Web-based resumes?

- A lot of technical people because they are familiar with the technology

- More and more professionals, including photographers, graphic designers, architects, and anyone whose marketing effort is enhanced by a graphic presentation

- Executives because it allows them to provide more detailed information about elaborate presentations, deals, operations, and creative proposals

Keep in mind: The content matters far more than the visual presentation.

How to Do It

A Web-based resume can be created in any up-to-date word processing program (Microsoft Word, Corel WordPerfect), a Web creation program (Microsoft FrontPage, Adobe GoLive, Macromedia Dreamweaver, Corel HoT-MetaL) or on many online locations (Tripod.com, Geocities.com) where you can post your resume.

- Begin with your basic resume.

- Review your resume to find significant items to highlight through hyperlinks. You may want to begin with six to eight bullet points of your strengths. You can create a hyperlink from each bullet point to its longer description in your basic resume or link it to additional material on another page.

You may also want to link to your educational accomplishments or to some significant projects you have worked on. One word of caution here: It is not a good idea to link to a Web site that takes a person away from your resume. For example, if you worked on a project for a company and they have detailed information online about that project, it is not recommended to link to that page. If the person follows that link, he or she may become so engaged in that page or the links that follow that they never get back to your resume site.

• It's a good idea to add hyperlinks at the end of each section that will give the reader the opportunity to go back to the top of your resume.

• Through the program you are using to create this Web-based resume, you can insert spreadsheets, graphs, sketches, photographs, and so on within the basic resume or you can link to separate pages. Make sure that anything you add enhances your resume and your marketing effort.

• Save your resume as an html (Hyper Text Markup Language) file. This is the language of the World Wide Web.

• When you have completed your Web-based resume, prepare a keyword summary. Do this by saving your resume to a text file. Reduce each sentence to one key word. Delete the duplicated words and any insignificant words until you have no more than 500 characters. Place a keyword meta tag at the top of your html resume like this:

```
<center><!—...[your list of meta tags inserted here]...>
</centered>
```

This is the information that search engines will look for.

• Creating this form of resume for the first time will take some work and practice. But it will soon become second nature to use this approach just as it has to use any other resume type. Because you can easily update your Web-based resume, it's important to keep it current. Review it regularly online and make changes as you gain new insight. Also, check all the links to make sure they work.

• If hiring managers like your resume, they will need to save it in some form—either printing it or saving it to their files. Again, make it easy for them. Keep your basic resume on a single Web page so that it can be printed easily. By the way, be sure to print it yourself after you have uploaded it to your hosting site to make sure it works and looks presentable. Also, try saving it as a text document. Then, open it and look at it to determine if all the important information comes across properly in the transfer process. These are the two ways hiring managers will retain the information, so make sure both work.

• Finally, once you have posted your Web site on a hosting site, promote your Web-based resume location by submitting it to search engines. Here are some places to start:

www.webthemes.com/submit.html

submitit.bcentral.com/

www.sitesolutions.com/

Use a search engine to find more options by conducting a search on "search engine submissions."

It's only logical that if we are talking about an online presentation we need to reference real online examples. So here are some valuable resources for you to use as you develop your own online marketing presentation.

Samples of Online Resumes

www.quintcareers.com/resume_samples.html

www.knowyourpet.com/resume1.htm

peterfmartin.home.mindspring.com/Full_Resume .htm

SIGNING BONUS: IS THERE A DIFFERENCE BETWEEN A RESUME READ BY A PERSON AND ONE READ BY A COMPUTER?

Yes. Most companies today use computer databases for storing and searching resumes. So when you send your resume to a company by e-mail you want to be sure it can be scanned or uploaded into the company system. Here are the guidelines.

- Keep the layout and format simple and clean.
- Avoid fancy formatting like italics, underlining, shadows, and reversed colors.
- Use common fonts like Helvetica, Courier, Arial, or Times.
- Font size should be between 10 and 14 points. The scanning process will reduce all fonts to the same size so choose one and stick with it.
- Do not condense spacing between letters.
- Set the length of your lines to eighty characters.
- Set left and right page margins at 1.25 inches to 1.5 inches.
- Use left-aligned margins.
- Do not use vertical or horizontal lines.
- Do not use a column format.
- Use all capital letters to set off sections.
- Put your contact information at the top of the page.

(continues)

Is There a Difference Between a Resume Read by a Person and One Read by a Computer? *(continued)*

Name
Street Address
City, State, ZIP
Telephone (if you have multiple numbers,
    put them on separate lines)
E-mail address
Web address for Web-based resume

- Use nouns, not verbs, to describe your qualifications. Searching is almost always done using nouns ("Designer" not "Designed and created publication").

- Load your resume with keywords related to your industry and focused on your specific strengths.

- Set your printer for high-quality printing if the resume must be printed and scanned. Many companies request the resume in electronic form (that is, by attachment or pasted into the body of the e-mail).

- Always send original prints rather than copies.

- Use white or light-colored paper.

- If you are mailing, be sure it is packaged carefully:

    Do not fold it.
    Use a white 9 × 12 envelope.
    Use a backing sheet of cardboard to support it.
    Write "PLEASE DO NOT BEND" on the
        envelope.

www.shawnclark.com/Resume/index.htm

www.wrconsulting.com/Software/Publications
/OkuntseffNik_v5.htm

Web Sites Where You Can Place Your Web-Based Resume for Free or at Low Cost

www.monster.com/

www.portfoliovault.com/

www.tripod.lycos.com/

geocities.yahoo.com/home

Tools for Preparing a Web-Based Resume

web.uvic.ca/akeller/e240/webexercise.html

www.paraben.com/html/rw.html. Paraben's
Resume Wizard is a resume publishing program
that publishes professional-looking resumes to
the Web, on paper, or as e-mail attachments. With
its wizard format, you don't have to be a professional desktop publisher to create a great-looking
resume. This updated version has added the ability to publish the resume in Word and to print directly from the program rather than from the html
document.

www.searchengineworld.com/misc/resume.htm.
Through a detailed Internet search, this is the
best article I found on how to create a Web-based
resume. It's fairly technical, but worth the effort
if you are serious about using the Internet in your
job search.

www.web-resume.org/. The Internet has revolution-
ized communication; now harness this power for
your job hunting. Web Resume Writer is a powerful
resume creation application for Windows 95/ 98/NT
designed to produce eye-catching resumes for paper

or the Internet. It offers a wealth of features to allow you to control the layout, appearance, and structure of your resume in a point and click environment. Publish your resume to paper, the Internet, or deliver it via e-mail.

mike.ceranski.com/software/RezInstall.exe. Create an exciting Web or e-mail resume in just minutes. More than 5,000 style, color, animation, and music combinations ensure your resume won't get lost in the crowd. Includes built-in spell checker, FTP services, and advice. One hundred percent freeware.

Tools for Keeping Track of Your Resume Postings and Job-Search Activities

Resume Tracker (http://shareware.lycos.com /tucows/files6/resumetrackerdemo.zip). This program is intended to help you with your job search. It tracks your job applications by keeping them in a database. Every application can be updated. This Resume Tracker

- prevents you from sending more than one application to the same person (e-mail address).
- allows you to have control over your job hunt.
- lets you see the whole list of applications along with their status (such as Interest, Interview, Wait, Rejected).
- can attach your resume or other documents to an application and track what has been sent.

CONSTRUCTING THE RESUME

Begin the process of building your resume by following the *functions-features-accomplishments-benefits* survey presented earlier in this chapter. Take plenty of time to do this to make sure you include everything in this list. Do this even if you decide to use a chronological, functional, or focused resume because it will give you the process for identifying the most important aspects of your background.

Once you have identified everything in your background of significance for marketing yourself, choose a resume form that fits your situation best and prepare a draft.

Construct the resume like a newspaper article. Each element is designed to pull you further into the story. Begin with the headline. This will probably be your professional summary in as few words as possible. You want something that is memorable that will cause the hiring manager to say, "That's interesting. I want to know more."

For example, I recently received a resume that said, "Experienced business development executive with demonstrated success selling products and services." This is short, engaging, succinct, and to the point. If the hiring manager is looking for that kind of person, they will read more.

Unfortunately, this executive went on to say, "and developing high performing sales and marketing teams for leading global hotel chains. Customer relationship management (CRM) consulting specialist, engagement manager, and practice leader with expertise in selling and implementing strategic, business transformational, technology-enabled, CRM solutions to global 2000 clients. Strategic alliance partnership developer and manager, skilled at implementing partner marketing and sales models. Innovative organizational 'intrapreneur,' with a proven track record of maximizing return on investment."

Whew! That's a mouthful. It may, in fact, be a good representation of his background, but how many hiring managers are going to sort through all of that stuff and attempt to apply it to their business and their immediate needs? Not many, I suspect.

You can make your headline an objective statement, but I don't recommend this. I believe it is too limiting to the job seeker. If you specify a job title as your objective, you may remove yourself from consideration for another job you are perfectly qualified to fill but has a different name. Job titles are so varied it is impossible to know all of the options. Also, if you seriously network, a job may be created just for you and you will get to create your own title.

The second section of your resume should include a bulleted list of your strengths that support your career goal (see chapter 3). It's important to use nouns, not verbs, to describe your qualifications since searches are almost always conducted by searching for nouns. This may look like this.

- Analyst
- Decision maker
- Self-motivator
- Communicator
- Salesman
- Creator
- Strategist
- Motivator

It is not necessary to demonstrate your knowledge and experience in these areas in this section. Remember, the goal is to pull the hiring manager/reader into your resume a section at a time. If the hiring manager is looking for the skills and experience that you have noted, he or she will continue reading to learn more. By the way, many times I see these bullet points in two columns or in tables. Do not do this because when the resume is scanned and converted to text, the list will become garbled.

The third section is where you begin to prove the claims you made in the first two sections. Take each item from your bulleted list, select a specific example from your work experience, and demonstrate your accomplishment in this area. You do not need to specifically identify the company where you accomplished that result.

For example, let's take the "Salesman" claim above. Here would be a good result statement: "Sold $7.5 million in CRM and custom software development business in nine months." Include the two or three strongest examples from your work history.

Section four is a list of your work experience that includes the last 20 years. It may look like this:

ABC Company, Anytown, USA — VP, National Sales, 1995–2001

You may include a short description of the business if it enhances your career goal.

Section five includes all of your education and training. Obviously, formal education is important. Also include all seminars, workshops, mentoring, and so on that enhance your background.

A section on personal interests can also be included. Here you might list your hobbies, public speaking you have done, special areas of interest. It is not a good idea to list very personal information, such as your spouse and children, your weight and height, your ethnic background, your church preference—these things cannot be considered in the hiring process and some hiring managers might protect themselves from this charge by excluding the resume from consideration. Also, do not include a photograph of yourself. Because a photo reveals information about ethnicity, gender, and age, it is illegal for an employer to require a photo.

Finally, do not include a statement like "References available." Everyone has references and so this statement simply uses space that can be put to better use.

Here are the things to remember:

- Show results. This is the single most important thing about your resume. Don't expect the hiring manager to connect the dots. You do it for them. Make his or her life easy.

- Start your result statements with an active verb ("created," "directed," "supervised," "managed," "planned," and so on).

- Create your resume with adequate white space. Too much content on a page makes it appear overwhelming. The eye needs white space to rest. You may feel you have such important content that it must be included. But remember, the purpose of the resume is to get the interview. So only include the information that will give you the best chance of getting that interview. You can elaborate later when you are talking one on one with the hiring manager.

Now that your first draft is complete, it's time to fine-tune your product. Start by assuming the role of hiring manager. Read your resume as though you are going to make a decision about hiring this person. Does the resume look inviting? Is it easy to read? Does it flow logically from point to point? Are all the questions answered that you would want answered? Are results demonstrated for every claim made in the resume? Is there a spark in the resume that makes you want to meet this person? Make the necessary adjustments.

Next run a spell check and a grammar check. I am amazed at how many people lay claim in their resumes to being a great writer, and the resume contains spelling and grammatical errors. You may not claim to be a great writer, but everyone at the six-figure level is expected to be a good communicator, and obvious errors do not strengthen your case. If you are weak in this area, get a writer or an editor to help you.

Now you are ready to get outside input. Ask people who know you well to review your resume. Ask them to be completely candid. Ask them the same questions you asked yourself in the review process.

- Does the resume look inviting?
- Is it easy to read?
- Does it flow logically from point to point?
- Are all the questions answered that you would want answered?
- Are results demonstrated for every claim made in the resume?
- Is there a spark in the resume that makes you want to meet this person?

Finally, you are ready to put it in front of people who don't know you well. Find some people you respect in another industry and ask them to review your resume, asking the same questions. Don't be defensive. Take the suggestions and criticisms and improve your product. One of the hardest things most of us ever have to do is to understand ourselves in a way that enables us to market ourselves as a product. Remember, you are worth it.

THE COVER LETTER

The purpose of the cover letter that accompanies a resume is to communicate how you fit a specific position. Never send a resume without a cover letter. This letter should be short and powerful.

First, identify the target position and assess the requirements for that position. This may be accomplished by reading the job opening announcement, the job description, or information located at the company's Web site. Research the company to learn about what they do, where they are located, their financial strength, and who the key players are.

Now it's time to draft the letter. The rules for cover letters are the same as for your resume. Each paragraph leads to the next, and it is your responsibility to give the reader a reason to keep reading.

Your first paragraph must grab the reader's attention within the few seconds it takes to scan the first two or three sentences. This is not a place to be cute or clever (although sometimes this does work); rather, it's a place to position yourself as a capable person who can do what the employer needs done. I recommend using your USP in your opening sentence—in a sense, your headline.

Demonstrate that you have done your research by addressing your letter to a specific individual and mentioning something specific about the company—recent acquisition, new product, or an award. State specifically what position you are applying for and why you are interested in this position.

The second paragraph is where you briefly describe how you are qualified. Call attention to education, training, and experience that are specifically related to what the employer is looking for. Don't overlook informal learning experiences or special interest projects that have enriched your education, skills, and experience.

Now you are ready to make your connection to the company—to demonstrate specifically how you can help the organization. Do not repeat your resume; use specific examples from your experience that demonstrate the value you can bring to this employer to accomplish specific things. You will know what these specific things are because you have done your homework.

Finally, tell the prospective employer how you will follow up. Say that you will call him or her in seven days to answer any questions. And, by all means, do it. You must always maintain the initiative in your job search. Never wait for someone else to call you. It's your job search, your life, and your responsibility.

And last, but certainly not least, be sure that all of your contact information (including your e-mail address) is included in your letter. If you have done a great job of communicating, have located the correct person to communicate with, and this company is looking for what you can do, you just may get a call. After all, this is what this entire process is about, so be a good Boy Scout and "Be Prepared."

CHAPTER 5

PLANNING FOR SUCCESS

lanning for success is a process, not an event. As an executive you already know the basics of planning. Starting with the goal, you back into the specific action steps needed to methodically progress from the present to the achievement of the goal, identifying the resources that will be needed along the way and the timeline required. Your goal this time is to find the right career position for yourself as soon as possible. This is where the planning you may be used to doing goes on the shelf. This particular project will be different for you, and not only because you're personally invested in the results.

Two primary elements are inherent in this project: high degree of uncertainty and different, sometimes opposing commitments, such as completion date, search costs, and scope of efforts.

You will need an effective mechanism for synchronizing your efforts without negatively affecting your efforts to find, qualify, win acceptance, close, or negotiate opportunities, since many of these activities may be going on simultaneously. This mechanism is your search plan. *Here* is where you start your planning.

Objectives: What is the major objective of this project? What are the final outcomes you want to produce? This is more than just writing down "Find a job." Describe the ideal job. Use your USP to help describe what this role looks like.

Deliverables: What are important intermediate milestones that you need to create in the process of achieving the major objective? How many networking contacts per week do you propose making? If it truly is an intelligent numbers game, what do the numbers need to look like in terms of letters, resumes, telephone calls, interviews, companies researched, and other basic job search activities? How do you plan to use the Internet and how does this translate into the number of hours each week you must commit to searching, posting, and contacting?

The statistics in figure 5.1 reflect a successful 27-week search conducted by a financial industries executive. She averaged one offer for every 204 contacts made. Based on her experience, if you ex-

Activity	Totals
Job Applications	395
Recruiter Contacts	214
Recruiter Interviews	32
Web Sites Posted	75
Networking	338
Employer Interviews	29
Blast Replies	575
	1658

37.8 contacts per week, excluding resume blasters

61 interviews total, or one per every 27 contacts, including resume blasters

61 interviews total, or one for every 16.5 contacts, excluding resume blasters

18 postscreening interviews, or one per every 56.7 contacts

5 offers, or one for every 12.2 total interviews

5 offers, or one for every 3.7 postscreening interviews

1 offer per every 204 contacts, excluding resume blasters

Interviews also counted as contacts

FIGURE 5.1

pected one offer per month you would have to make 50 contacts each week to produce the number of interviews that would result in an offer. How would you schedule your time each day in each week to achieve this milestone?

Success Criteria: What are the constraints within which you must work? What weekly milestones make sense for you? Are there inviolate conditions imposed upon the approach you take that may limit your time or resources? What are the boundary conditions of the search environment you must consider, such as geographic or targeted-industry limitations? What does success look like along the way?

Once you have sketched out the objectives, deliverables, and success criteria for your search project, you can drill down thoroughly into the details and organize your work in a way that supports your efforts toward achieving the goal of finding that new six-figure-income job. Revisit these planning factors each week to determine if they have changed and adjust your detailed planning accordingly.

CREATING A DETAILED SEARCH PLAN

There are a number of things that need to be ready before you execute your search. These are forms and other documents you will use to communicate with employers and recruiters or as tools to help you search efficiently. Some of these tools can be developed now, others later as you build your search plan. Let's begin with a list.

- Resume
- Cover letter format

- Unique Selling Proposition (USP)
- Networking contacts
- Web site posting list
- Search engine list
- Forms

  Daily do list

  Contact reporting

  Recruiters contacted

  Employers contacted

  Networking log

  Search plan overview (see figure 5.2)

In all probability, your search will take much longer than just six weeks. However, the first six weeks are crucial to setting things in place, establishing a routine, and fine-tuning your system. We will start here and describe each item in reverse order.

Daily routine established: If you are not a part-time job seeker looking for new opportunities while still employed, you need to work at finding a job just like it was your job, from 8:00 A.M. to 5:00 P.M. with

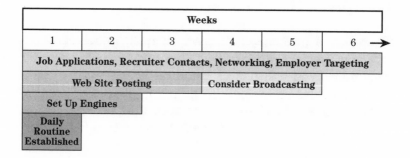

FIGURE 5.2: Search Plan Overview

a half-hour lunch break. Establishing a daily routine in the first week of your job search is important. If you procrastinate in the first week, you will probably procrastinate throughout your search. Set the pattern right the first time. Interviews, networking appointments, attending meetings of professional organizations, and other search-related activities will help to break up the routine nicely.

Set up engines: You will read later about job agents that are search engines inside of many of the executive employment Web sites to which you will post your resume. These use criteria you determine to search job listings and send you their results via e-mail. This multiplies your search efforts and invariably turns up opportunities you can apply for online.

Web site posting: You will find employment Web sites, recruiter Web sites, and employer Web sites that will allow you to post your resume for recruiters and employers to search. Even though you will continue to find sites like these throughout your search, most of the ones you choose to post on will be identified in the first few weeks of your search.

Consider broadcasting: Broadcasting refers to using resume distribution services or direct mail services for contacting recruiters or employers respectively. After the first few weeks of searching, you will have developed a feel for the job market, established your system, and worked through all the opportunities that were available when you first got on the Internet. Now it is a matter of a daily check for new postings. Based on your experience, you may want to evaluate the various distribution services available and their fees. This may be a good way to spread the net further.

Job applications, recruiter contacts, networking, and employer targeting: These are activities you will engage in every day. You will continue to find new jobs to apply for, new recruiters to register with, new contacts to network with, and specific employers you will want to target for resume submission or networking. As you can tell, the first two weeks in the preceding illustration are full of activity, four each day for a while, according to the Search Plan Overview!

Some people like organization. They will jump on this project right away and have a system ready to go in a day or so—Mr. Organized! Others are not so organized and will not realize how much help a system is until they have several hundred contacts of all sorts to keep track of. Paper everywhere! Who to call back? Where is that e-mail address? Did I send them a resume already? What did I say in that cover letter? How long has it been since I followed up? A system helps. There's no getting around it. It doesn't have to be this one; you can invent your own. This will help you get started. The bottom line is simple: Keep track of what you are doing. (See chapter 4, page 82, for Resume Tracker software program.)

Now is a good time to sit down and map out your search plan.

1. Write out your objectives, deliverables, and success criteria.
2. Determine what your practical milestones should be.
3. Create a table similar to the one illustrated in figure 5.2, but be sure yours covers at least twelve weeks (the first three months).
4. Write your milestones under the appropriate week.
5. Fill in the other activities.

6. Give it a reality check—can you effectively accomplish this in the time allotted?

You will see several examples in this chapter of how this is done. Again, the important thing is that you *do* document your detailed plan—the method can be whatever works for you.

DEVELOPING A TRACKING SYSTEM

There are a number of forms you can develop to help you keep track of progress and results.

Networking Log: Keep track of those you network with—when you talked with them last, what about, and how to get in touch with them (see figure 5.3). Note the contacts you want to add to your Life List, those you want to continue to network with even after your search is complete and you have your new job.

This can be done on paper, though the best method is on your computer so that you can sort by name, company, or date when you need that specific information. Something like this normally is done in the spreadsheet function of your software, but some word processing software programs afford that option as well. These illustrations obviously do not provide the room necessary for all the information. Set up your forms with plenty of room.

Employers Contacted/Jobs Applied For: You will be contacting employers as a function of targeting as well as responding to job postings. Keep track of the employer name, job applied for (if any), contact name (if any), address, telephone numbers, and date (see figure 5.4). You may prefer more information or even

Name	Company	Addresses	Phone Numbers	E-mail	Date Contacted	Topic

FIGURE 5.3: Networking Log

Employer	Job Application	Addresses	Contact Name	Phone Numbers	Date
Micro	No—broadcast	123 etceteras	Mr. Hire	123-456-7890	mm/dd/yy
Handy Dandy	VP Sales #429	456 etceteras	Ms. Recruit	987-654-3210	mm/dd/yy

FIGURE 5.4: Employers Contacted/Jobs Applied For

less information. Work with the system for a while and then customize it to your style. Again, the computer is the best place to keep the list for the same reasons. You can always print out a hard copy if you need one.

It is a good idea to print out a copy of the job description and your cover letter (hard copy or e-mail) and file them together by date. Employers and recruiters often respond to you weeks after you submitted your information. A quick sort on the computer under recruiter or employer will quickly identify the company involved. Then it is a simple matter of checking the date, going to that chronological place in your filing system, and pulling the information you need to remember what in the world you sent them and what you said. As you develop different versions of your resume and customize your cover letters it will become more and more important to be able to retrieve information on the specific job or contact and how you represented yourself.

Recruiters Contacted: You will identify recruiters to submit your resume to on the Internet as a function of searching for them as well as responding to job postings listed by recruiters. Keep track of them—firms, names, telephone numbers, e-mail addresses, why you contacted them (see figure 5.5). Even if they do not match your resume to a job, they will keep your resume on file. You may want to contact some of them in the future depending on the nature of your first discussions. Some you may want to add to your networking list.

In figure 5.5, Chris Cromwell received a blind resume. If Chris Cromwell calls with a position to discuss, how are you going to keep track of it? Yes, this becomes a new entry on your Employer/Jobs list. Notice that Tommy Tender is a corporate recruiter.

Recruiting Firm	Phone Name	Phone Numbers	E-mail	Nature of Contact
Getajob Inc.	Chris Cromwell	123-456-7890	Recruiter@email	Sent blind resume
Hathaway LLC	Tommy Tender	987-654-3210	TT@hath.email	Corp. recruiter
Hitech	Frank Fodder	None Given	ff.recruit@email	Resume Blast

FIGURE 5.5: Recruiters Contacted

SIGNING BONUS:
ANALYSIS OF A SIX-FIGURE SEARCH GRID

Six-figure job searches typically take an average of nine months to produce the right job. Obviously, some searches take much less time and others, much more, usually with one or more offers turned down by the executive along the way.

Using the material in this book, executives have successfully concluded their search in as little as nine weeks and as long as 27 weeks, still well below the average. Again, this is a range that will change with the job market and does not constitute a norm. It is simply a snapshot in time. Figure 5.6 shows the record for the executive who found a new position in 27 weeks.

Blast replies refers to telephone, e-mail, or auto-reply confirmation of receipt of electronically distributed resumes. In actuality, the distribution reached more than 11,000 employers and recruiters. The practice was discontinued for several reasons, including the observation that time was better invested in focused searching where measurable results were far improved. There were no hardcopy distribution services utilized; resumes and other material changed hands in face-to-face interviews. In other words, snail-mail was not used in this search.

Patterns in the numbers of contacts each week vary considerably. Holidays occurred in some weeks. Interview preparation kept the executive off-line for longer than normal in weeks where multiple interviews were scheduled. This particular executive also developed a number of legitimate short-term consulting engagements during the period covered by the search.

Activity	Week 1	Week 2	Week 3	Week 4	Week 5	Week 6	Week 7	Week 8
Job Applications	22	13	18	9	15	10	28	19
Recruiter Contacts	20	26	15	8	10	8	31	29
Recruiter Interviews	0	5	2	0	2	2	0	2
Web Sites Posted	21	7	6	5	4	6	4	3
Networking	11	7	9	13	15	14	9	17
Employer Interviews	0	1	1	1	1	1	1	2
Blast Replies	0	387	0	0	0	186	0	0
	74	446	51	36	47	227	73	72

Activity	Week 9	Week 10	Week 11	Week 12	Week 13	Week 14	Week 15	Week 16
Job Applications	15	20	9	30	14	11	8	18
Recruiter Contacts	4	5	3	21	1	4	3	4
Recruiter Interviews	2	1	0	0	2	1	1	0
Web Sites Posted	1	1	2	2	1	0	1	1
Networking	10	6	13	13	15	15	8	17
Employer Interviews	2	2	1	1	0	3	1	1
Blast Replies	0	0	0	0	0	1	0	0
	34	35	28	67	33	35	22	41

FIGURE 5.6: Twenty-Seven-Week Search Grid

(continues)

ANALYSIS OF A SIX-FIGURE SEARCH GRID

(continued)

Activity	Week 17	Week 18	Week 19	Week 20	Week 21	Week 22	Week 23	Week 24
Job Applications	13	18	18	10	12	12	14	14
Recruiter Contacts	5	2	2	4	1	4	3	0
Recruiter Interviews	1	1	2	1	0	3	1	0
Web Sites Posted	2	0	0	2	1	1	0	1
Networking	11	8	15	12	12	9	36	26
Employer Interviews	0	1	0	2	1	0	0	1
Blast Replies	1	0	0	0	0	0	0	0
	33	30	37	31	27	29	54	42

Activity	Week 25	Week 26	Week 27	Totals
Job Applications	9	13	3	395
Recruiter Contacts	0	1	0	214
Recruiter Interviews	0	2	1	32
Web Sites Posted	0	2	1	75
Networking	7	5	5	338
Employer Interviews	1	0	4	29
Blast Replies	0	0	0	575
	17	23	14	1658

37.8 contacts per week, excluding resume blasters

61 interviews total, or one per every 27 contacts, including resume blasters

61 interviews total, or one per every 16.5 contacts, excluding resume blasters

18 postscreening interviews, or one per every 56.7 contacts

5 offers, or one for every 12.2 total interviews

5 offers, or one for every 3.7 postscreening interviews

1 offer per every 204 contacts, excluding resume blasters

Interviews also counted as contacts

Resume blasters discontinued due to lack of response

Four offers were extended during the process of the search and were turned down for various reasons beginning in week eight. The offer that was accepted in week 27 began with a screening interview in week 16, an 11-week process. During that period of time, the position was on hold for three weeks. Eight weeks, the net length of time this candidacy lasted, is not an unusual length of time for a senior management role. Many senior executive searches last longer.

Postscreening Interviews as a statistic refers to face-to-face discussions with an individual who has the authority to hire. The difference between total employer interviews and postscreening interviews is represented by multiple interviews with the same employer recorded in the table but counted only once in the summary following.

The position accepted was that of chief operating officer for a major division in a $3 billion parent company. Compensation included a base salary well into six figures, bonus, and deferred compensation. Figure 5.7 shows some other helpful comparisons.

Notice that networking constituted 33 percent of all contacts and resulted in 60 percent of all postscreening interviews. The job this executive landed began as a networking contact developed from a value-added relationship established with a professional executive recruiter. The recruiter put this executive in touch with someone inside the company and was not involved in the search at all. At the time, there was no position available. However, this executive maintained a value-added relationship with the inside networking contact as well. When a need emerged that this executive was qualified to fill, guess who got the call?

Only one postscreening interview developed from contacting 395 employers directly about open

(continues)

ANALYSIS OF A SIX-FIGURE SEARCH GRID

(continued)

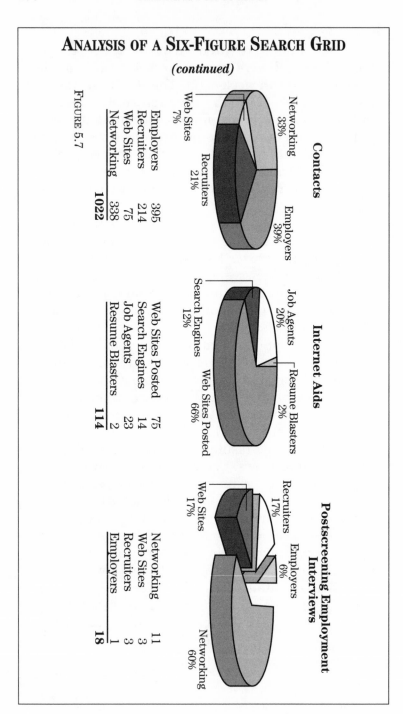

Contacts

Networking
33%

Recruiters
21%

Web Sites
7%

Employers
39%

Employers	395
Recruiters	214
Web Sites	75
Networking	338
	1022

Internet Aids

Search Engines
12%

Job Agents
20%

Resume Blasters
2%

Web Sites Posted
66%

Web Sites Posted	75
Search Engines	14
Job Agents	23
Resume Blasters	2
	114

Postscreening Employment Interviews

Recruiters
17%

Web Sites
17%

Employers
6%

Networking
60%

Networking	11
Web Sites	3
Recruiters	3
Employers	1
	18

FIGURE 5.7

positions. This does not mean a six-figure job seeker should avoid contacting employers—in the intelligent numbers game, any qualified contact you can make is important. Three interviews resulted from employers finding the executive's resume posted on a Web site and three more from recruiters they had registered with. All of these are important, but the job seeker must adjust expectations in terms of results. Networking is still the best game in town.

He works for Hathaway LLC. A search for that company name will not turn up on your Employer/Jobs list unless you enter the information there as well. It is always helpful to search both Employer/Job lists and Recruiter lists when you are trying to reconstruct a contact you made in order to retrieve specific information from your files. Frank Fodder responded to your recruiter broadcast. You will get calls from your broadcasting efforts both to discuss a particular job and to screen you more thoroughly to keep you in their database. You will also get auto replies. If these contain the name of the recruiter and the e-mail address, you may want to touch base again in the future just to see if anything has come across their desk lately.

Contact Reporting: Tracking your search statistics will help you identify progress, set realistic weekly goals, and identify what is working best for you (see figure 5.8). You saw this form in chapter 2.

The executives involved had a goal of 50 contacts per week among employers, recruiters, and networking. Most weeks they hit their goal. This chart, maintained on a spreadsheet, also provided the basis for their accountability for progress. In order

Activity	Week 1	Week 2	Week 3	Week 4	Week 5	Week 6	Week 7	Week 8	Week 9	Week 10	Totals
Job Applications	22	13	18	9	15	10	28	19	15	20	169
Recruiter Contacts	20	26	15	8	10	8	31	29	4	5	156
Recruiter Interviews	0	5	2	0	2	2	0	2	2	1	16
Web Sites Posted	21	7	6	5	4	6	4	3	1	1	58
Networking	11	7	9	13	15	14	9	17	10	6	111
Employer Interviews	0	1	1	1	1	1	1	2	2	2	12
Blast Replies	0	387	0	0	0	186	0	0	0	0	573
	74	446	51	36	47	227	73	72	34	35	1095

FIGURE 5.8: Search Activity Statistics

to better understand what the numbers were telling them, they extracted certain information to evaluate separately: the various origins of employment interviews, the different types and number of contacts, and the types of Internet aids used (see figure 5.9).

Employment Interviews here refers to post-screening interviews. In all, this executive had 28 interviews with recruiters and employers, but only 10 of them were after the initial screening interviews, when they were legitimately in the candidacy process. Most of these came from networking, even though networking represented fewer contacts than either employer or recruiter contacts. Broadcasting to recruiters, in this instance, produced 573 telephone, e-mail, or auto reply contacts (out of approximately 6,500 contacts) but was the least effective in leading to postscreening interviews—zero.

With the 700 Rule in mind, the executive took out broadcasting numbers to get a better feel for legitimate contacts. Web sites were counted each time a recruiter or employer indicated they were responding to a posted resume. Notice that the total count

Employment Interviews		Contacts		Internet Aids	
Network	5	Employers	169	Web Sites Posted	58
Web Site	2	Recruiters	156	Search Engines	14
Recruiter	2	Web Sites	58	Job Agents	12
Employer	1	Networking	111	Resume Blasters	2
Total	**10**	**Total**	**494**	**Total**	**86**

FIGURE 5.9: Origin of Interviews, Contacts, and Internet Aids Used

is slightly fewer than 500 at week 10. Somewhere in the process, the 50-contact-per-week goal was missed. It is also obvious that building the numbers takes time.

Tabulating the Internet aids helps identify which resources are producing the most contacts and interviews. The suggestion in all of this is not that you keep track of everything so that you can generate tables and charts. The suggestion is that you review your numbers weekly to see if they are telling you something that may help refine your search efforts.

Daily Do List: This begins with establishing your daily routine. Here is one suggestion.

1. Check your e-mailed search engine responses and respond accordingly.
2. Scan your posted Web sites for the most recent job postings and respond accordingly.
3. Search for recruiters to contact using your generic search engines.
4. Search for employer Web sites for job postings and information that will enable you to send a cover letter and resume.
5. Search for more employment sites.
6. Make networking calls.
7. Make follow-up calls to employers and recruiters. This will be tough in many cases, since only e-mail information may have been provided and the employer not identified in the job description. However, there will be enough to keep you busy.

Your do list is built at the end of each day for the next day. Throughout the day you will add to the do list as you receive calls and e-mails and find other contact information you want to follow up on. If you have kept your notes complete on the do list, it also becomes the source of information for updating all your various lists at the end of each day.

USING YOUR TIME

Some of us can't stand the rigors of planning beyond sketching out a few items on a do list or stuffing reminder notes in our calendars. Other people really groove on planning and can take it to the extreme. A plan will help you be effective. Only you can determine the right balance in your circumstances between a veritable paper hell on your desk and so many forms, charts, graphs, lists, and process diagrams that you waste valuable time maintaining your plan.

When planning use of your time, here are two things to consider:

1. Business moves very fast these days.
   - Search sites every day and respond immediately to new postings. Postings are generally filled long before the posting subscription runs out.
   - Check back with recruiters and employers often, since positions can appear and disappear quickly based on changing business conditions for employers.
   - Be patient with employers. Many have long internal hiring processes that can become more prolonged related to these same business factors.

2. Planning has a purpose.
   - Your search plan should anticipate immediate action on your part.

- *You* should be in control of your search plan, rather than control ending up by default in the hands of recruiters, employers, and the vagaries of the job.
- Your search plan will need to be adjusted regularly if you are going to get optimal response to your efforts.

Your results will directly reflect how you use your time and the disciplined effort you make to build your plan, adjust your plan, and execute your plan on a daily basis. You may be tempted to view your search plan as a set of procedures and checklists that will guarantee you will find the right job as quickly as possible. Not true!

Your search plan is a systematic approach to finding a job you have designed and customized to your own circumstances and needs. Its purpose is to help you be effective in your search efforts, and it will help prevent you from wasting time, including from spending time on the wrong things.

As a highly qualified seasoned executive you may also be tempted to think that a great plan means you will get picked up right away. Not true! It is true that there are more than 8 million six-figure and higher jobs out there. However, each of those executives is strongly committed to keeping their jobs for obvious reasons. The average highly paid executive takes about nine months to land a new position. You may be fortunate and find something sooner or you may be among those that take longer. The best response to the timeline dilemma is to work hard and smart, and that is what a good search plan and efficient use of time make possible.

You may want to spend more of your time broadcasting your credentials using electronic and snail-mail distribution services in hopes it will speed up the job search rather than spending the time in a more focused search. Again, not true! This is a subtle point. The reason you cast a big net is to get the numbers working in your favor in terms of the qualified leads you turn up. However, indiscriminately distributing your resume is like blasting away at a distant target with a shotgun while a more focused search is like using a rifle with a powerful scope to zero in on the target. The process takes the same amount of time whether you use the shotgun or the rifle method. The focused search statistically is going to produce better results. The advantage of the shotgun method is in evaluating the results—who is responding and why.

This is not advice to avoid broadcasting methodology, just counsel to keep your expectations realistic and to use the shotgun method in balance. Proportionally, your time is better invested in a focused search.

The time that counts is how long it takes to turn leads into interviews and interviews into offers. This takes much longer for the six-figure executive than for the average job seeker, in large part because of the extra care exercised by employers in their process of evaluating candidates for significant positions. Use every means at your disposal to turn up qualified leads quickly, but keep in mind that volume does not always translate into less time.

You may think, "Hiring an executive coach or outplacement firm is all I need to do. They will find me a job, and I can spend my time doing other things." Not true, but sooner or later this thought will occur to you! Executive coaches and outplacement firms can help you be effective in your search, but their role is not to find a job for you. That is your job. In some cases, their resume review services, marketing services, and coaching processes may take even longer than if you tackled these tasks yourself. They have a limited staff serving more than just one individual at a time and you are subject to the inherent speed of their infrastructure. There are other avenues to use in obtaining this kind of help that may be less time consuming. Always inquire about process time in the course of evaluating offline resources you may want to use. And remember: Always take control of your life.

Another timesaving thought you may have: "My network is extensive, and it should not take long to secure a new position." Not true! Networking *is* the most effective means of turning up job leads and getting in front of the right people. However, your connectedness is largely unrelated to job market realities. The state of the economy will impact your timeline to a much greater extent than the size of your network. Many executives we have helped in slow economies have shared a similar experience: They were the top candidate all the way through the interview process only to find out the job was put on hold, went away altogether, or their candidacy was discontinued because relocation became a financial obstacle for the employer.

Nevertheless, it was networking that got them in front of a decision maker who made the decision to hire them. It just couldn't change the economic factors that put following through on that decision out of the question. Keep the funnel full of opportunities in process until you get the nod you want and it's a sure thing. This means time spent networking is a valuable investment and should not be sacrificed unnecessarily for other activities as a shortsighted time-saver.

You may think recruiters are time-savers as well because they will introduce you to prospects. Not true! This does happen more often in a booming economy and with less highly paid positions. Keep in mind, though, that executive recruiters are usually retained and are developing likely candidates for their client with a specific job in mind. It does help to get into their stable and to maintain cordial contact with executive recruiters, as they may be retained for a search in the future that you are qualified for. It is easier for them to pull a resume out of the file than to initiate a new search from ground zero. It is worth spending the time to contact targeted recruiters and develop cordial relationships with some. Find meaningful ways to stay on their mental front burner, but don't rely on their efforts on your behalf to buy you time in executing your search plan.

Keep in mind that your search plan is dynamic, changing with your experience as you systematically work through the process of a job search. Don't crucify yourself when the plan doesn't produce the results you thought it should. Think it through. Is this a burp along the way? What is going on in the market that affects my plan? Should I make some adjustments to the plan or perhaps to my expectations? Don't be afraid to dump or change something that isn't working for you. It's your plan. You can adjust it whenever you want. It is one of your best tools, and you need to keep it oiled and sharp.

CHAPTER 6

THE HIDDEN
JOB MARKET

The U.S. Department of Labor states that 85 percent of all jobs are never advertised. Think about it—*85 percent*. Furthermore, the help-wanted ads in the classified section of newspapers represent only about 10 percent of all jobs currently available. Given these statistics, it quickly becomes obvious that if you limit your search to advertised jobs you are only one-tenth as effective as you have the potential of being. Networking, personal marketing, relational selling, and research are the crucial tasks you need to perform in order to unlock this market. Well, then, just what and where is the hidden job market?

The opportunities you need to know about must be mined, like gold out of the earth. A good prospector knows what signs to look for and where lies the most likely place to dig. Discovery takes effort, much of which turns up nothing. But conducting an informed search increases the likelihood of turning up that one nugget. You are prospecting for job opportunities, and you need to conduct an informed search. Understanding why these opportunities are hidden will help you know where to look.

These jobs are just under the surface of your search for a number of very good reasons.

1. High-level positions are often filled by an employer using a retained executive search firm. These firms usually recruit from currently employed executives, their own network, a databank of resumes, and other professional resources. You won't find these jobs posted on a Web site or advertised in a trade journal or newspaper.

2. Employers will often post positions on their company's Web site. This is a convenience to the employer. In an effort to fill the role through networking or internal placement, interested job seekers can be directed to this Web site to obtain more information about the job. Unless you have a specific reason to visit their Web site or stumble across it accidentally, it is unlikely you will know about this opportunity.

3. Employers often search informally before pursuing a more traditional search. This means they use their own networks with customers, suppliers, friends, colleagues, and employee referrals first. This can happen before their human resources department has been made aware of the opening. At times, this is for convenience. At other times, it may be the need for confidentiality.

4. The position may have been vacated so recently that formal processes for communicating this opportunity may not yet have kicked in. If you can learn of positions soon to be vacated or recently vacated before the recruiting process has gotten off the ground you can minimize the competition.

5. Some companies actually prefer filling top positions only through networking. The personal recommendations of other top executives become the primary deciding factors when it comes to identifying candidates.

6. Company policy or regulatory compliance may require an employer to post an opportunity internally. This may be the only place the job appears in print.

7. Recruiters working for employers maintain their own databases of likely candidates. Often this means there is no need to publicize an opportunity. Their own resources are sufficient to find qualified candidates.

8. Many recruiters use Web sites specifically dedicated to their industry and search these databases exclusively.

9. Some jobs are waiting to be discovered, even by the employer. A major pharmaceutical company had divested its interests, and the new company acquired another pharmaceutical company. In the process, its supply chain became confused and ineffective. One of my networking contacts was looking for a new opportunity and knew the parent corporation's senior executive recruiter. In discussing this problem one day in the course of just staying in touch, my contact suggested the company needed a senior vice president of supply chain management to clean up the mess and manage its supply chain. In the end, a position was created for this executive that had not existed before.

As you can see, there are many reasons jobs remain hidden from the normal view of likely candidates. But the jobs are there, and this hidden job market represents an opportunity to find or create a position to fit your unique qualifications. However, it is going to take a bit of prospecting to discover these opportunities.

How can you tap this market? To find the needle in the haystack requires refined search skills and know-how. Though the basic elements remain the same—contacting employers, meeting recruiters, and networking—the manner in which these elements are performed and the emphasis each receives is radically different for the executive than it is for other job seekers.

Recruiters and networking take on new importance in this highly compensated niche. This puts a priority on maintaining value-added contact with executive recruiters, particularly retained-search recruiters. Many of these maintain their own private networks, and keeping in touch as a function of your networking strategy in general can pay off. Touching base periodically with CEOs, COOs, and general managers in your growing network is important as well. Many of the top jobs are known only to recruiting firms retained to execute a high-level confidential search and to senior executives well connected in the industry.

There is no magic bullet. The basic steps are the same whether you are looking for a $45,000 job or a $245,000 job. Just keep in mind that you're not looking for a tennis ball in a haystack—you truly are looking for a needle in the haystack.

You may want to consider resources such as www .execunet.com. This is an effective fee-paid Web site designed for six-figure executives. Using your search engines will turn up more sites to check out. Beware of the organizations that tell you they have hundreds of highly paid jobs waiting to be filled. They may have been retained to fill a six-figure position, but it is more likely they find out about these opportunities the same way you do. One way to tell is by how much they charge. One well-known executive search agency wanted an executive candidate to pay in excess of $20,000 for help with their search. The free material they sent described a process that really didn't offer anything the candidate couldn't do or have done at a much lower cost. If this candidate had been an extremely busy executive financially supported by the generous outplacement program of a former corporation, it might have been a different story. Most of us do not have that luxury, and this executive certainly did not either. He declined.

There are a few Web sites that focus on six-figure jobs that allow resume posting and job search. These include:

www.6figurejobs.com

www.garage.com

www.boardseat.com

www.bigwigs.net

Some executive recruiting firms, like Korn/Ferry, Leaders Online, and Heidrick & Struggles, maintain their own searchable Web sites that enable posting as well. Again, your best tool for locating recruiters and Web sites that focus on highly paid executives is your search engine.

Web sites focused exclusively on highly paid executives contain jobs that only members can browse. The jobs are hidden from those making less than six figures—they cannot qualify as a member, free or paid, and therefore cannot search the site. You have to qualify as a bona fide highly paid executive and sometimes pay a membership fee to use these sites. Though this is to your advantage, don't forget that these jobs are not hidden from the other six-figure job seekers, your competition. Fortunately, there is more that can be done to research the invisible job market than networking, contacting employers directly, and maintaining your retained recruiter connections. There is also list mining and stratospheric contact generation.

List Mining

The availability of jobs above the $75,000-per-year level decreases exponentially. Above mid–six figures, they can be carried in a basket. The challenge for the executive is how to uncover these jobs, most of which are handled by retained search firms or the company itself without ever appearing on the visible job market. It is still important to use the Internet; evaluate advertised positions; post on appropriate company, recruiter, and executive Web sites; and engage in all the other activities that put your credentials out there where they can be discovered. You may score a hit, but keep in mind this is a long shot. Your best bet is to capitalize on your networking skills.

Your goal is to talk to a hiring manager in an organization that needs what you have to offer. Since there are thousands of companies that might fit that requirement, the task may seem overwhelming. So start by simplifying the process. Identify 20 target companies and conduct thorough research to find that one key person to speak with. That research can be done at the public library or on the Internet. After you have developed your skill and expertise in researching these 20 companies, add another 20 and keep going until you find that perfect six-figure opportunity that is just right for you.

One way to develop a target list of companies to contact is to use Internet mailing lists or discussion groups. This may lead to uncovering hidden jobs, making a new networking contact that may lead to a job opportunity in the near future, or developing a relationship that results in a job being created for you. There are a number of sources out there to consider:

www.hoovers.com/compant/lists_best.com

www.tile.net

www.lists.apple.com

www.lsoft.com

www.topica.com

These are just a few to get you started. They provide various search capabilities to mine for company and contact names. A good Internet research tool is Alexa (www.alexa.com), a kind of "reverse search" engine. This tool, which needs to be installed on your computer, finds Web sites that are related to the topic you are searching. For example, if you find that one of the sites above is valuable, say, www.topica.com, Alexa gives you a list of sites that are similar to topica.

Use your search engines to identify other potential list-building tools. Here are a few to consider using and why.

Yahoo—the largest subject-organized search engine

Virtual Library—organized like a library index

Trade Wave Galaxy—trade information

Google—the largest linked search engine

Alta Vista—best for single-word or -phrase searches

Search.com, Profusion, Ixquick—all-in-one sites

Another source of company and contact names that is worth mentioning again is professional publications—general business publications, trade association publications, and industry reports. Use your preferred list builder to identify these professional publications, then use your search engines to scour for details. You are looking for professional contacts who are in a position to know of viable job opportunities as well as professionals they may know in the same position.

Niche or vertical sites are particularly valuable. These Web sites focus on specific industries or skill sets and make it possible to locate jobs you may be targeting that fit within that vertical orientation. They may include:

- Accounting jobs (www.accounting.com)
- Finance jobs (www.nytimes.com/pages/jobs/jobs _finance/index.html)
- MBA jobs (www.mbajobs.net)
- Health management jobs (www.health managementjobs.com)

They may also include association Web sites such as:

- American College of Trial Lawyers (www.actl.com)

- Association of Fundraising Professionals (www.nsfre.org)
- Society of Manufacturing Engineers (www.sme.org)
- American Marketing Association (www.marketing power.com)

Besides the specific job announcements on these sites, there is a wealth of industry information that will lead you to key people in these industries. Read the news stories and glean names and contact information from them. Then, follow up by finding the specific information you need in order to contact each person.

STRATOSPHERIC CONTACT GENERATION

Now for the million-dollar question: How do you turn company and contact names into addresses, telephone numbers, and e-mail addresses? It is one thing to identify the highly placed executive to talk to and quite another thing to nail down just how to pull this off. Is snail-mail the best approach? a telephone call? an e-mail? How can you identify an approach that is going to go right to the contact? Ideally, an e-mail address should be used because it bypasses so many potential gatekeepers.

Start by identifying the company's Web site if they have one and it isn't listed in any of the material you mined out of the Internet. You are looking for the domain name where the Web site is located. The domain name is the information that follows the @ in the e-mail address. As you move from left to right in the address after the @, the size of the organization increases. In conducting a somewhat blind search on the Internet it is difficult sometimes to identify the difference between a small sole proprietorship that will not have likely opportunities for you and a larger corporation. One clue to size is the number of periods in the extension. jdoe@acme.itt.com is an indication John Doe works for a large corporation, while jdoe@acme.com may just be a three-person sole proprietorship. For example, name.nasa.gov represents the name of a Web site at a particular company or unit within NASA, which is one of many government entities.

There are a number of directories you can use to search for domain names for companies. Here are a few:

www.iaf.net

www.checkdomain.com

www.concentric.net

www.usethenet.com

www.four11.com

www.altavista.com

Of course, you can use your search engines to find more. There is no one single composite directory, and you may have to use several to find the site address you are looking for.

Addresses and telephone numbers are the easiest to find, using www.whitepages.com or www.yellowpages.com. E-mail addresses can be a little trickier. E-mail addresses have two parts. The e-mail name, also called the user ID or e-mail ID, precedes the @, and the e-mail domain name follows it. There are some e-mail address directories you can try in addition to the more general domain search tools just mentioned.

Yahoo's People Finder

Mesa—Meta E-mail Search Agent

Switchboard

WhoThere?

e-mailman

In the end you may just have to guess, but even this can be done intelligently. Many companies have their e-mail set up to hunt for the closest address if they receive an e-mail that is close but no match for any specific listing. And because the domain name frequently is the company's name, two approximations that often work are:

firstname.lastname@domainname.com

firstname_lastname@domainname.com

You can also try the first name only or initial and last name structure that is also widely used.

firstinitiallastname@domainname.com

firstname@domainname.com

You can always call the company and ask for its company Web site address, company e-mail address, and even the e-mail address of the individual you are attempting to identify. If you can only obtain a company e-mail address, be sure you mark your e-mail to the attention of the appropriate individual *in the subject line.* Many times this will be forwarded to the identified person without question. Often the "contact us" page on a company's Web site provides a general e-mail address as a place to start.

You can also search the Internet for general company information using your search engines. Here are a few sites you can start with. Each of these sites offers other links and free services as well as fee-based services. Be sure to read the conditions of use carefully.

www.corporateinformation.com

www.virtualchase.com

www.nypl.com

www.companysleuth.com

A sales and marketing executive ran out of networking contacts. She used list agents to compile a list of trade journals and other publications dealing with the golfing industry. Then she searched for articles dealing with recent mergers and acquisitions. The articles she found turned up several companies, and the chairmen of the board were identified in the articles in each case. The online yellow pages provided the company names and addresses. An online directory search turned up the company Web sites, and the sites included the companies' general e-mail addresses. The e-mail addresses for the chairmen were not on the site and did not turn up in the online search of e-mail address directories.

The executive did two things. First, she e-mailed a cover letter and resume as a single document to each company marked for the attention of the chairman of the board by name and title. Second, she experimented with e-mail addresses in an effort to send the same information directly to the chairmen of these companies. In all three cases, the first effort resulted in a "bounce-back"—wrong address. On the second try, she nailed it for two of the chairmen. She never did get the address for the third. A telephone call to the company did not help.

The good news is that *both* the company and direct e-mail for one of the chairmen made it through to the right person. There was a need for a new vice president of world marketing in one case, and after a relatively short process, this executive got the nod.

HOW TO REACH THE HIRING MANAGER

Once you have identified your target company, you contact the hiring manager. But what if you don't have the name of the hiring manager? It is very important to address your contacts to a specific person. Here's how you do it.

Call the company's main switchboard and ask. Say, "Hello. My name is _____." (It's very important to identify yourself. People are reluctant to give out information to strangers. I find a good sense of humor is also very helpful in establishing rapport.) "Can you tell me who is in charge of your _____ department?" (Specify the department you are interested in reaching— marketing, finance, whatever.) The goal is to get the person's name so you can send an introduction letter.

The second step is to send a letter of introduction, including your USP, and a general description of what you are looking for. Indicate that you will call on the telephone within 72 hours. (The length of time you state is not all that important because you can't possibly know when the letter will actually be delivered, but it demonstrates decisiveness and commitment.) And then be sure to call.

When you call you may reach the hiring manager directly, and this is good. Be ready with your dialog. Say, "Hello, this is _____. I found your name _____, and I am impressed with _____ (whatever reason caused you to call this person). I sent you my resume, and I am interested in _____ (doing whatever it is you want to do). Do you have a few minutes to speak with me now?"

Secretaries, Assistants, and Other Gatekeepers

We all know about the gatekeepers—those dedicated folks who protect us from the onslaught of the outside world and who keep us from getting in. They are not bad people. It's just that an important part of their job description is to protect the person they are working for from disruptions that keep him or her from using time in the most effective way. And the better they are at their job, the more difficult it is to get to the hiring manager you want to speak with.

So develop a plan to work with them rather than against them. Begin by being courteous. Ask for his or her name—many salespeople are not going to be as courteous, and the gatekeepers are on guard for salespeople above all others. And be sure to make a record of the name because you probably are going to have to do this again and again in many different offices. Visit with the person to establish a positive rapport and to get on friendly terms. Ask for information about the company, the hours of operation, and where they conduct business. Try to determine if the person you are trying to reach is the correct person. You don't want to waste time calling and calling and calling only to learn much later that you have reached the wrong person. Gatekeepers can help you. In turn, offer to help if the opportunity presents itself. Treat them like they are the most important people in the world. Right now, for you, they are.

Then, call persistently at different times of the day. Many hiring managers answer their own telephones when the gatekeeper is away. So be prepared to speak directly with the hiring manager whenever you call because you cannot know when that moment will come. Never leave a message for them to call you. They will rarely call back and when you initiate another call, everyone will be on the defensive. So, as with everything else in the job search—maintain the initiative.

While you are working to make a frontal attack through the gatekeeper, keep your eyes and ears open for a third-party referral. Try to find someone who knows the hiring manager you want to talk to and arrange a meeting with that person. Then, use the new contact to acquire a referral to the original person. Nothing is more powerful than networking among friends.

Voice Mail

You cannot control what happens to you, but you can control your response to it. And this applies to voice mail. When you are all ready to have an important conversation with a hiring manager and you get voice mail, it can be a huge letdown. You have to quickly decide whether to leave a message or hang up.

My suggestion is that you be prepared to leave a message—but not just any message. Plan ahead. Recognize that you are going to get voice mail a lot, so have your message ready to go. When preparing your message, include your name, the purpose of your call, and your main USP. Leave your telephone number, but don't ask the person to call you back. And when you leave your number do it slowly and distinctly. Give the hiring manager time to write it down. I usually repeat it twice because I have had too many experiences where people have left their number but the sound is garbled for one digit. It takes a lot of guessing to find that missing digit.

When you call a second time, have another message ready. This time emphasize your second-strongest USP. And keep the process going until you talk to the hiring manager or you decide to stop the process.

It's also important to follow up every call with a personal handwritten note that you mail through U.S. mail. Be sure to reiterate the message you left on the voice mail. Can you see that this type of persistence will be recognized and eventually the hiring manager is going to want to talk to you just to find out what makes you tick?

What to Do When the Hiring Manager Needs More Information—Objections

One of the biggest reasons people don't make telephone calls is because they are afraid the hiring manager is going to raise an objection. The reality is that in nearly every case, you can be sure the hiring manager is going to raise an objection—because you are looking for a job and, in most cases, they don't have a job to offer.

So if the problem is that you don't think you'll know what to say when objections are raised, the solution is to accept that challenge and figure out what to say. There are only so many objections that can be raised. Record them when you hear them. If you can answer the objection on the spot, of course you will do that. But if you do not have the answer the first time you hear the objection, take the time to find the answer. Practice saying it over and over again until it becomes natural. Now you are ready to go again. Each time you hear a new objection, record it, find the answer, and practice it. In no time at all, you will become a pro.

Some of the objections you hear might include these.

- *We are not hiring now.*

Your answer: "Great. The reason I am calling is because I know you are an expert in this area of business, and I am looking for other people to speak with to learn more. This will only take a minute."

- *Send me your resume and I'll look at it.*

Your answer: "I've already sent you one." Or "I'll be glad to do that. But let me just take a minute to tell you what I do [your USP]."

- *I don't have time right now.*

Your answer: "I understand you are very busy, and I'll only take a minute of your time." Have your short USP statement ready to go when you get the go-ahead.

There is no truly hidden job. Someone, somewhere, knows about the job or is aware of the need. An enterprising candidate can turn this fact into opportunities. Your search skills and using your network and the Internet make the difference. This takes patience and effort. It is not the easiest task you face in your search efforts, but by following these ideas and suggestions, you *can* infiltrate the hidden job market.

Just like the old prospector who had a clear vision of what he was working for, you can be sure that "thar's gold in them thar hills."

Chapter 7

The Art of Networking

Your next job will almost certainly come from someone you know. The problem right now is that you probably don't know enough people. What do you do about that?

The answer is really quite simple: Meet more people. However, because you want to get back to work as quickly as possible and in the *right* new position, it's important that you meet and talk to the right people.

A few years ago I was in a job transition and needed a job. I had learned from previous experience that networking is the most effective way to find a new opportunity. So I prepared a very short list of five of my networking contacts. Out of those five interviews, I turned up three bona fide job opportunities. I took one of the jobs and turned another one into a new client for the company I went to work for. Not bad results for so little effort. It was possible because I had kept my network alive and well through regular cultivation.

ASSESSING THE MARKET—
WHO DO I WANT TO TALK TO?

Who are the right people? The easy answer: the highest-level person you can get to who has the authority to hire. It's a funny thing about human nature. We almost always refer down, not up. A CEO will often refer you to a president or a senior vice president; a president will refer you to a senior vice president or a vice president; a senior vice president will refer you to a vice president or a manager. And so on. It's important to remember this because it's one of the main reasons you should always start as high as possible in the corporate hierarchy.

You may have a neighbor or a close relative who is a manager or director at that ideal company. Should you talk to them and ask for referrals? Absolutely! They probably won't be able to get you in front of that top-level manager, but there's always a chance that they can. So, don't ever pass up an opportunity. Talk to them. Find out what they know about the company. What's the corporate culture? What do they know about product cycles or projects in the pipeline? Who do they know in the organization? Even if they are unable to put you in front of the significant players, once you know who the players are, you can look for people who know those people and can make the introduction.

I have often made the comment, "Nothing is ever wasted." We don't know who someone else knows. Some of my best long-term contacts have come from the most unlikely sources. Also, some of my best business has come from unlikely sources. I try always to take the time to talk with anyone who wants to talk to me. I don't do it for self-serving reasons. I do it because I genuinely care about people. But experience has shown me that many, many times good things come from taking the time to talk to people.

There is one group of people you must never talk to: the human resources staff. Never go to the human resources department (unless, of course, you are a human resources professional)! It is a waste of time! You will fill out forms. Your resume will go into a stack—either literally or figuratively—*and you will never hear from them again.* It is extremely rare for a six-figure executive to be hired through the human resources department.

Building Your List

The key to coming up with names is some sort of relational connection. Business people you have interacted with, suppliers you have done business with, colleagues you have worked with, other members of professional organizations, contacts in companies you have given business to, former coworkers now working somewhere else; the list goes on. Networking is not just talking to family and friends.

Most people know about 200 people. To begin the networking process, set up a three-column list (figure 7.1). Head the first column "Name," the second, "Position," and the third, "Level of Acquaintance." Enter the name of every person you know in the Names column. You will probably fill up several pages. Don't prejudge the people on this list. Write down every person you can think of as quickly as you can write. Ask yourself:

> What contacts are in my address book?
>
> Who is in my rolodex?
>
> Who did I work with in my last position and the position before that?
>
> Who were the suppliers to these companies?
>
> Who were the customers?
>
> What attorneys do I know?
>
> What accountants do I know?
>
> What insurance agents do I know?
>
> What doctors do I know?

SIGNING BONUS: USING ONLINE BOOKSELLERS TO INCREASE YOUR CONTACTS

There is an expression that says, "You are what you read." Look at your own bookshelf. Can a person get a pretty good idea who you are by looking at the titles of your books? Could you get a pretty good idea of who another person is by looking at his or her bookshelf? We may not be able to look at the real bookshelves of some of the authorities in our career field, but we may be able to look at their virtual bookshelf.

Go to Amazon.com (www.amazon.com) and do a search for a topic in your field, say, "compensation and benefits." When I did this search, the top three results returned were *Human Resource Management, Establishing a System of Policies and Procedures,* and *Peopleware: Productive Projects and Teams.*

Let's take a closer look at *Establishing a System of Policies and Procedures.* By clicking on the title or the book cover image you are redirected to a page containing more information about this title. You're looking for an item called "Customer Reviews." When you click on that item, you see that (as of this writing), there have been 21 reviews written, and the first one written is by Linda Zarate. She not only read the book but cared enough to write a review about it. She is ranked as a Top 100 Reviewer, which certainly means that she has reviewed a lot of other books as well. Click on the link "Linda Zarate (see more about me)."

Here you see that she has written 173 reviews. In this case, a list of review categories is included to organize the information that is available. You can click on any category and be taken to her reviews for that category.

In that same profile box, you will find an Add button, which you can press to add this person to your "favorite people" list. If you have an account with Amazon you can add any reviewer to your favorite people list. Later you can upgrade this person to your "friends" list, which will reveal the e-mail address, if previously hidden.

There may be more information about this person by clicking the "more" button in the profile. This will open up a larger description about the person and her interests. In this case her "more" information says, in part:

> Co-developer of the Tarrani-Zarate Information Technology Management Model and 25-year veteran of the computer industry.
>
> Recently moved my home page to www.tarrani .net/linda/. If you share interests in IT operations, service delivery, and process engineering you're welcome to check it out. Also see my two weblogs at http://ZarateTarrani.blogspot.com/ and http:// Postcrds.blogspot.com/ and my Women in IT forum at http://forums.delphiforums.com/WomenInIT/start.
>
> My personal mission in life is to help others as a means of repaying those who have opened doors for me, helped me to achieve, and inspired me to be the best in my personal and professional life.

The e-mail address is provided, so if this is someone you would like to network with, send an e-mail, using the guidelines above, and open the door to a new network area.

Continue to explore the Internet for new techniques in information gathering. It is already a goldmine of information. I learned this idea from Shally Steckerl (shally@jobmachine.net), who is CEO of Job Machine, Inc., in an article he wrote that was on the Web site ERDaily (www.erexchange.com). Who knows where it will go in the future?

What real estate agents do I know?

Who do I know from church?

Who do I know from sporting events, either my own or my children's?

Who do I know from the college I attended? (Look through your yearbooks.)

Who do I know from professional organizations?

Who did I meet at the last convention I attended?

Who do I know who is currently (or was recently) looking for a new job?

Who are the experts in my field? (See the Signing Bonus on page 136.)

Who wrote the professional books I have read?

Keep your list handy and be ready to add to it as you think of other people. Once you start this process, you will be amazed at how many additions you will think of as you go through your day.

The second step is to review your list to identify the people who hold top positions. In the Position column, enter each person's title: CEO, president, vice president, manager, director, and so on. If you are going to sort this list by computer it's a good idea to assign priority numbers to each position: CEO = 1, president = 2, etc. If you don't know everyone's title, do some research to find out. Every person has some title, and it's important to know what it is. And what are the job responsibilities of the people on your list? If you don't know, it's research time again.

In the Level of Acquaintance column, assign a rank to each person that reflects how well you know him or her. Use a scale of 1 to 5, with 1 being a very close relationship and 5 representing someone you barely know.

Now it's time to organize the list for action. First sort the list based on how well you know the person. Second, sort the list by title. This establishes your priority for contacting the people on your list. You want to talk to the highest person on your list that you know best.

SETTING UP THE INTERVIEW

Now you are ready to contact the people on your list. Send a letter by U.S. mail or e-mail. Be candid. Tell your contact that you are looking for a new career opportunity. Tell him or her that you are in the process of networking to increase your knowledge and understanding of the marketplace. You are asking for help. Most people are willing to help another person as long as it doesn't cost them something. It's important to recognize this.

Name	Position	Level of Acquaintance

FIGURE 7.1: Networking Grid

Here is an example of an introduction letter that I recommend:

Dear _____:

I am in the process of looking for a new career opportunity. I have great respect for your knowledge of the economy in our city, and I would like to spend 30 minutes with you in order to learn from you.

I want you to be assured that I am not coming to ask you for a job or even if you know of a job that is open. I am simply coming to learn from you.

Are you available next Wednesday at 10:00 A.M.?

I am enclosing a copy of my resume. I would appreciate it if you could review it in order to help me improve my presentation. Specifically:

- Is my professional summary clear, specific, and to the point?

- Are my accomplishments easy to understand?

I will call you on Friday to confirm this appointment. Thank you for your time. I look forward to talking to you soon.

Sincerely,

John Doe

Enclosure

There are some important points in this letter.

In the first paragraph, state specifically why you are contacting them: 1) because you are networking to find a new career opportunity and 2) because you have respect for their knowledge. Always give them a sincere compliment related to the reason you want to speak with them. I maintain that there is always a reason to give a sincere compliment. If you cannot do that, then there is probably no reason to spend time talking to that person.

In the second paragraph, it is very important to state as clearly as possible that you are not asking them for a job or even if they know of a job. Remember, almost everyone is willing to help as long as it doesn't cost them anything. People like to say yes and do not want to tell you no. Most people you network with will not have a position to offer you. You do not want to put them in the uncomfortable position of having to say, "No, we don't have any openings at this time." You want to make it easy for them to say "Yes, I would be happy to spend 30 minutes with you."

In the third paragraph, ask for an appointment at a specific time. Most of the time the person will suggest an alternate time, but it's important to be decisive. And, of course, it's important to be on time. It's equally important to honor your request for 30 minutes and to offer to leave when the time is up. I say "offer to leave" because many times the person will want you to stay longer. That's great. It's what you would like to have happen, but it must be their choice and not yours.

In the fourth paragraph, mention your resume. The purpose of enclosing your resume is to get them thinking about you. The reason networking is so effective is because the only way a person can really understand who you are and what you can do is to process you through his or her own organization.

As you sit in front of these people, they are asking themselves, "How could we use a person like this in our company?" You don't have to ask them if they have a position for you in the company because they will be doing the asking for you.

In the fifth paragraph, maintain the initiative in your job search. Take responsibility for confirming the appointment. It demonstrates your strength, decisiveness, and ability to get things done. These are qualities that companies hire.

THE INFORMATIONAL INTERVIEW

There are three goals to accomplish in this interview:

1. Meet the person, if you have not previously met, or renew the acquaintance.
2. Learn everything you can about the person, his or her business, the industry, and how you might fit in the industry.
3. Ask for referrals to three additional people to talk to.

Control the Interview

When you arrive at the interview (a few minutes early) be ready to take control. And how do you do that? By asking questions. Many people believe the way to control an interview is by doing all the talking. Wrong. When you do all the talking, you may, in fact, say too much and the wrong things. Remember, you are there to learn—not to impress.

What questions do you ask? Here are some to get you started:

> In reviewing the material I provided in advance, did you find the summary (objective, goal) in my resume clear? Have I made it clear what I am trying to accomplish? (This forces your contacts to start to process you through their organization, which is the only way they can really understand you.)
>
> What does your company do?
>
> How did it get started in this market?
>
> What is the business outlook in your industry?
>
> How long have you been in business?
>
> How large is this market?

Is your business local, regional, national, or global?

What are the future opportunities for your company?

When a position similar to what I am looking for is to be filled in your organization, what does your recruiting staff look for?

If you could choose one quality you wish employees had more of, what would it be?

Whom do you suggest I talk to for constructive insight regarding my search or who may be aware of other opportunities I should pursue?

What industry sectors do you feel are growing the most at the moment?

Does your company expect to grow in the next five years?

What is the biggest challenge you face right now?

How do you plan to solve this?

How did you get into this industry?

Where did you get your training?

Did it prepare you for what you are doing now?

What is the best experience you ever had in business?

What was the most challenging thing that ever happened to you?

Can you see how a person with my background would fit in your industry?

What opportunities are there in your industry for a person with my background?

What would the career path I'm interested in look like?

What kind of compensation would a person in that position expect?

What skills are you looking for in your business?

How would a person develop those skills?

Are there Internet or media resources you are familiar with that I should consider using in my search?

Of course, the person you are interviewing will ask you questions as well. My advice is to be prepared to answer the obvious questions. Some of these questions may be included.

What are you looking for?

What is your ideal job?

What have you been doing?

What is it that you do?

Why did you leave your previous place of employment? (Do not ever bad-mouth your former employer even if you think they deserve it.)

Where are you concentrating your search?

Who have you talked to?

How can I help you?

Put yourself in their place. What would you want to know about someone who called you for networking? Write those questions down. Other questions will come up in your conversations. Add questions to your list that get asked a lot and that are particularly insightful. Rehearse your answers.

In order to maintain control of the interview, answer questions succinctly and completely and immediately follow up by asking another question. If you answer a question and stop, you invite another question from the person *you* are interviewing. It then compels you to answer and you've lost control. Remember, you are there to learn, so maintain control and ask questions.

This process often seems counter-intuitive when you are starting out. We tend to go into our "selling mode" to impress people with how much we know. Act like a medical doctor. Ask questions. Listen. Gather information. Then diagnose. When you spend all of the time talking, you are, in effect, diagnosing before you have the facts.

If you handle these interviews properly, the people you interview will think you are a great conversationalist because you let them talk about their favorite subject—themselves and their company. They will be impressed when you provide answers that are "on target."

And how do you do that? Through active listening.

Active Listening

There may be no skill that is more valuable than active listening—the process of focusing on the speaker, processing what is being said, and testing your understanding.

Figure 7.2 shows the four basic types of conversationalists.

Clearly, most people will be a mix of these types with one aspect tending to predominate. This suggests you should weight your responses toward the dominant type but not ignore other responses available to you.

When you are first engaging in your networking conversations, study this chart and be a careful listener. Tailor your responses conversationally, based on the responses you get to your first few questions.

Many people are more intent on what they are going to say next than what is being said to them. If this description fits you, then you will need to practice listening. When you are in a conversation with another person, focus on his or her face. Looking right into the eyes can be unnerving to you and the person you are in conversation with. However, if you focus on a spot between the eyes and slightly above, you can comfortably engage the speaker without creating discomfort for you or the speaker. Now, mind you, I am not advocating that you fix on that spot and never divert your gaze. Rather

Type	What They Look For	How You Should Respond
Aggressive	Action to take The bottom line Solving problems Getting results Taking control	State the objective up front Don't interrupt Ask about pros and cons Give direct answers Be prepared
Collaborative	Articulation People issues Enthusiasm Opportunity to help Participation	Stay focused on the subject Be sincere and genuine Take a logical approach Express gratitude Seek facts
Disciplined	Consistency Patience Special skills Listening ability Demonstrated success	Be flexible Express appreciation Minimize use of their time Respect traditional ways Demonstrate competence
Qualitative	Attention to standards Compliance Key details Familiar circumstances Critical analysis	No wild ideas Stay on track Quality of your efforts Ability to make decisions Precise search objective

FIGURE 7.2: The Four Types of Conversationalists

think of it as a "home base." Occasionally, look directly into the eyes of the person or glance away. However, never give the impression that you are looking around the room for someone else to speak to—a better offer.

We have all had experiences where we are in conversation with a person and that person looks past you as though you suddenly disappeared. How did that make you feel? There is nothing more important in this interview than to connect with the other person. Several years ago my wife and I attended a very large church. We were not very active in the church and so were not well known. At the conclusion of each service, the senior pastor would greet people at the door. Every time I spoke to him at the conclusion of the service, for that moment in time, I felt like I was the most important person in his life. He firmly shook my hand, looked me in the eye, thanked me for coming, and wished me well. This was a great lesson for me, and I have continued to practice this engaging style with everyone I speak to because, in truth, that person is the most important person to me in that moment. Why would I waste my valuable time speaking to someone who had no worth? I believe that every experience talking with people of any status in life is a valuable experience—for me and for them. I can learn from anyone if I approach the conversation with an open mind. Therefore, that person is valuable to me.

It's not enough to simply focus on *what* is being said because the goal is to fully *understand* what is being said. While listening, think about what is being said— not about what you will say next—and how it works. Connect the dots. Follow the process that is being laid out for you. If you don't understand the point that is being made, ask for clarification. I will often say, "This is what I understand you are saying," then summarize and play it back to them in my own words and ask, "Do I have this right?" People are never offended if you ask for clarification because it shows that you really care about and want to fully understand what they are saying.

Finally, after the speaker has concluded the topic, test your understanding by suggesting a scenario that uses the information. Apply it to your own situation, a fictitious example, or, best of all, to their situation. Of course, you won't always have it just right, but your contacts will be impressed that you cared enough to get involved in what matters to them.

There is a simple rule in life: People buy from people they like. People also hire people they like. And when you demonstrate that you are genuinely interested in what matters most to them, they are going to like you, too.

Next Steps

Frequently in the course of the interview, names of other people come up. The person you are interviewing often says, "You should talk to this person." Of course, when that happens, be sure to get the correct spelling of the name and the contact information. I have found that the longer I can keep people talking, the more people they think of for me to talk with.

If no names come up during the course of the conversation, ask for referrals before you leave. Simply say, "Who else should I talk to in order to continue my investigation?" By now the person you are interviewing knows quite a bit about you, and your question will trigger names of people who might be helpful to you.

I cannot stress this too much: The old saying "Birds of a feather flock together" holds true in the business world. So if you are interviewing a president of an organization, he or she probably has other friends who are presidents and those are the names you'll walk away with.

As soon as you get the contact information for a new person you want to interview, you send another letter or e-mail. Now you simply change the first paragraph of your letter to say:

> I was visiting with your friend, John Doe, and he suggested I contact you. I am in the process of looking for a new career opportunity. John tells me he has great respect for your knowledge of the economy in our city, and I would like to spend 30 minutes with you in order to learn from you.

You have never met this person, and without the introduction, he likely would not be willing to give you 30 minutes. However, because he values his relationship with his friend, he will give you the half hour as a favor to his friend. I use this networking approach every day, and it consistently works. Of course, I make cold calls, too, but I much prefer these warm calls. The conversations are easier to start, the quality of information is better, and the opportunity to get referrals is increased.

By now you can see that networking expands in an exponential rather than a linear fashion. If you are serious about this endeavor and aggressive about its implementation, it is not very long until you are overwhelmed with potential contacts. This is a very good thing. Now you have an opportunity to be selective and choose only the very best people at the highest levels to interview.

MID-COURSE CORRECTIONS

As you conduct your interviews you will begin to receive feedback about your presentation—your written materials (resume and cover letters) and your oral communication (questions, answers, and content). This gives you an opportunity to make adjustments as you proceed.

Before you began this informational interview process, you developed a professional summary. Now, based upon the feedback you've received, you will probably decide to adjust it. As you learn more about a variety of industries and types of positions, you will decide you are no longer interested in some. That's a very beneficial part of this process. When that happens, move potential interviews in that category to a lower priority. Do not take them off of your list entirely because there may be a time when it makes sense to talk to them.

Constantly assess where you are in the process. Make adjustments. And keep talking to as many people as you can. This process works every time without fail. As you can see, it's a simple process. It's the same process that you use in business every day—prospect, cultivate, and ask.

You can use this same process to make cold calls. However, it is much easier and more effective to network through the referral process. It is essentially an opportunity for a friend to help a friend with very little risk involved.

IS IT WORKING?

At this point, people often say, "But this is a slow process." And they are correct. It does take time to do this. However, remember that the average time for a six-figure professional to acquire the right new position is nine months. If you look at networking in that context, it is not too slow. And if you take the broader view and look at networking as growing your database for future development, the time you spend networking is invaluable.

We all want to accomplish our goals quickly and easily. Thus we look for the quick and easy ways to do this, the obvious ways, like looking at the classifieds, talking to human resource departments, filling out applications, and sending resumes. And sometimes these approaches work. So do everything you can do to find a new position—but make networking your number-one priority. When you've done all the networking you can, then it's time for some of the other approaches.

As stated above, there are only three main goals in this networking process—get to know the person, learn all you can, and get more referrals. If you accomplish that, you have been successful. However, from time to time, one of these networking contacts will refer you to someone who does have a position that may be of interest to you. And sometimes your contact has a position that might be of interest to you. Your contact may even tell you that although the company doesn't have an appropriate position open, the organization could really use your skills and experience and maybe a position could be created for you. Wow! That's the best of all worlds. Since we all try to make our work fit our personality and work style, to find a position that is tailor-made for us has to be the epitome of job success.

These things really do happen, and that's the immediate purpose of networking. But they are the exception, not the norm, so it's very important to keep the hopper full. If you have only one situation you are working on and it falls through, you are going to be very disappointed because 100 percent of your opportunities just evaporated. However, if you have 100 situations in process and one falls through, you have lost only 1 percent of your opportunities and you still have a lot of hope in your burgeoning hopper.

The networking you're doing now is for a very specific purpose—to find a new job. As I continually stress, however, what you are building is an enormous lifetime resource. You are meeting people now who may become sources of valuable business intelligence, business partners, even good friends.

Years ago, when Bill Clinton was a fledgling politician, he began to accumulate names on index cards. He made notes about people and continually cycled back to them, keeping the contacts alive and well. As he progressed in his career, this resource became the backbone of his political success. Clinton understood the importance of a network and never gave up on keeping it alive and well.

This is what I am encouraging you to do. And when you think of the tremendous opportunity you have during this time of transition to build this network, your perspective will change. It will no longer seem like a slow process; rather, you will be wishing you had more time to build this incredible resource.

EXECUTION

You may struggle through your first few calls until you get the hang of it. Many of us are uncomfortable calling "strangers," a little embarrassed about our situation, and reluctant to impose on people. These feelings are all quite normal and part of the roller coaster every job seeker rides.

One issue in particular can be challenging. How do people feel about your age? It is easy enough to create a resume that does not directly reveal you are a mature job seeker, insulating yourself somewhat from age discrimination. But in interviews and while networking, that is more difficult to accomplish.

A key factor is to make age a positive and not be defensive about it. In every opportunity, age can be a positive or a negative depending on the level of experience the opening requires. And when you get to the point of seeing people face-to-face, talking and connecting, age becomes a moot issue. By focusing on your contributions—past, present, and future—you will learn to enjoy the conversations. So will the potential employers— older workers are famous for being among the most productive employees available on the market.

I have also found that the way your voice sounds on the telephone can be a tremendous asset or negative factor in handling the age issue. I have had many people remark that they think I am 20 years younger than I am based on phone conversations. When they meet me in person they are surprised to find that I am older than they expected. But by then it doesn't matter because we have already established a positive relationship.

If you don't have a naturally "young-sounding" voice, work on getting one. It isn't a matter of having a thin, high-pitched voice that sounds like your voice hasn't changed yet or a cute, little-girlish sound. It's a matter of energy, enthusiasm, ideas, and good questions. You *can* acquire a young-sounding voice. As with most things in life, ask those around you to help you and be open to their suggestions. It's very difficult to see ourselves as others see us.

Whether your networking appointment is via telephone or, preferably, in person, *don't be late!* Those we network with are essentially volunteering their time to help us. That is something to be respected. It should be treated like an investment that will grow in value over time. Be sure to leave your contact information, including your e-mail address, and let your contact know that you have a good feeling about the conversation, that you learned a lot, and that you really do appreciate their time. They may just invite you to call again in a few weeks or give you a call out of the blue one day with a new lead.

Keep Good Records

Who have you talked to? What further leads did you generate? When did you follow up on them? What did you talk about? Should they be added to your Lifetime Networking List? Where does this suggest you focus your effort? Are your network contacts spread across multiple industries or concentrated in a single one? Have any of them asked you for further information, a referral to someone to help them, a piece of business information? When did you respond? Did you thank them before, during, and after the conversation? Part of successful execution is knowing what you've done so you know what you need to do next. You should answer all of these questions, and maybe others, about each of your networking contacts.

Use your Lifetime Networking List every week to stay in touch with those people you want to network with regardless of your employment situation. If people ask you to keep them posted on your progress, even if they are not on this list, do just that. Remember that they have made an investment in you. We all like to know how our investments are doing. The goal is to be talking to people all day, every day, about things that matter to your job search.

Execution is about getting it done. All the preparation is wasted and all the insights regarding relational selling are of no use if you don't send that letter or e-mail or don't pick up the telephone and call someone. Networking puts you on the firing line without a job posting or an invitation to submit a resume acting as a buffer. However, networking still remains the fastest way to uncover opportunities.

A Practical Guide for Staying in Front of People

Since you are building a lifetime resource, you certainly want to treat it the right way from the beginning. So as soon as you can after your face-to-face interview, write a thank-you note. It is impossible to overstate the importance of thank-you notes. Tom Peters in his little book, *The Pursuit of WOW!* (New York: Vintage Books, 1994) states:

> Don't forget your thank-you notes! You just read the most important piece of "advice" in this book. If you take it to heart, you can throw this little volume in the nearest trash can and still have gotten ten times your money's

worth (make that ten thousand times). The power of a thank-you (note or otherwise) is hard—make that impossible—to beat.

In your thank-you note, provide a brief description of your career aim by way of a reminder of the value you bring to an organization. Share your plans for pursuing the leads they gave you and assure them you will keep them posted on your job search. Remember, this is a mutual relationship. If you can give something back of value, do so.

To write a thank-you note following the first interview is essential; I believe it is also the absolute minimum. When your new contact takes 30 minutes out of his life to visit with you, he or she has invested in your life. As with any other investment, this person would like to know how it is paying off. So tell them. Be creative and find ways to stay in touch with them.

As an executive search consultant, every day I talk to many clients, prospects, and candidates. Unless I do something immediately to stay in contact with them, in most cases I will forget who they are. Now, mind you, it isn't because I want to forget them or choose to forget them; I just cannot keep that much information in my mind. The other day, a very well-qualified person called me and indicated he was interested in finding a new opportunity. While talking to this person I made a mental note to keep in touch with him. The next day I saw his name on a list and could not remember who he was or what I was supposed to do for him. Fortunately, I had made a permanent record of our conversation and after reviewing that record, I was able to recall how I wanted to work with him. As your ever-expanding network continues to grow, you will begin to experience the same phenomenon.

E-mail is a terrific way to stay in touch with people. It is rare to find anyone in today's business world who does not have e-mail. It is also rare to find an e-mail inbox that is not overloaded with messages. There are some important guidelines to follow to avoid becoming part of the unwanted bulk.

- A monthly update is usually adequate unless you have a news flash to share.

- Treat the subject line as a "headline." Remember the advertising rule and answer the question, "What's in it for me?" (Be sure to answer this question from the point of view of the person who will be reading the e-mail!) Don't make outlandish or misleading claims, but do suggest in the subject line the value that is contained in your e-mail message.

- Keep it short. Use easy-to-understand verbiage and short, readable sentences. Use white space between paragraphs.

- Check your spelling and grammar. I'm amazed at how many people leave out words and use incorrect grammar and spelling. And these are the same people who claim to be sticklers for detail and great communicators.

- Always, always, always include a signature block that contains every possible way you can be contacted. What if the person wants to call you and tell you about a great opportunity he just heard about, but can't figure out how to contact you? You must make it easy to find you.

I have a contact—I would call him a friend although we have never met in person—who sends me an e-mail every single weekday. I don't mind getting this e-mail. In fact, I asked him to "put me on his list" because he is sending me something of value. I first met him when he was looking for a new position. Unfortunately, I was unable to help him at the time but he started sending me a daily devotional. I enjoyed the publication and asked him to keep sending it to me. Now, I think of Walt every single day. Whenever a great opportunity comes up that fits his skills, interests, and background, he is the first to know.

I believe this example is an exception. I don't think it's necessary to provide an update every day but it represents a creative solution. (I'm not sure Walt really understood how valuable this was at the time he started this.) He never talks about himself, his interests, or his desire to find a new opportunity, but he is always there in my mind. What creative thing can you do to stay in front of your contacts on a monthly basis? Can you think of an interesting way to update them on your search progress? What information do you have that might be of value that could be presented through a monthly e-mail update? This is definitely worth your time to develop and will set you apart from 99 percent of your competition.

It is up to you, the job seeker, to keep your name in front of your contacts. Expecting that they will somehow magically remember your name if a suitable opportunity surfaces is leaving too much to chance. You have to call them back, but not without a valid reason. The goal is to talk to them again and make a connection in their mind regarding your search.

You can separate your employer, recruiter, and networking candidates into two lists. Call the first list "Contacts." Use this list to keep track of every single contact you make. Include when you made the contact and a brief note about what was discussed. Even though it may be unlikely you will recontact some of these folks, the list will help you reconstruct the timeline and context when someone on the list happens to call back out of the blue. Label the other list "Live." These are people you intend to call back at reasonable intervals, say every two or three weeks, to stay in touch. The criterion for adding someone to this list is very straightforward:

- Was the rapport positive in your conversation?
- Did the contact indicate a willingness to try to reach you should an appropriate opportunity arise?

- Did you receive an invitation to touch base again in the future regarding potential opportunities that may come up?
- Were you asked to call back?

If the answer to any of these questions was yes, add that person to the list. You can call these people frequently at reasonable intervals to keep them updated on your search and inquire about any new job opportunities, people to network with, or other leads.

DEVELOPING THE REPUTATION AS A VALUE-ADDED CANDIDATE

Here is a unique way of securing a callback invitation. Ask your contacts what jobs they are seeking to fill at the moment. If you know something about the job category, and more important, someone who might qualify, follow with another question: "What is the single most important requirement or qualification for that job?" Finally, mention that you may know of someone who has those qualifications. Would they like a referral?

No one ever turns down an offer of help—a result of the tyranny of the urgent. You can contact the individuals that came to mind and ask their permission to pass on their information for this position. After a week or ten days call your contact again, remind him or her of who you are and provide the information. As other people come to mind later on, you can call again. What you are doing is creating a value-added impression connected with your name. Of course, be wise enough not to pass on unqualified referrals.

In many of your conversations the party on the other end will bring up one business issue or another. Offer to find and provide some information on the topic if the other party is interested in receiving it. Be careful to suggest this only when you have or know where to find the bona fide information. Sometimes it may be a book recommendation and where to find it. Sometimes it may be an article remembered from the Internet. You get the picture—if you are a "value-added" potential candidate, you will have no trouble getting invitations to call back.

As you network, opportunities of interest will begin to appear and it will be important to be ready to promote your candidacy through relational selling.

Chapter 8

Relational Selling

Relational selling is an issue of leadership. Sound strange? Well, look at it this way: Management is about things and lining up the right resources at the right time to get results. Leadership, on the other hand, is about people and influencing them to act. You want to influence recruiters and, ultimately, an employer to act on your behalf—specifically, to offer you a job. It is your initiative, not theirs, that gets the ball rolling.

That takes leadership. And not just any leadership—it takes the kind of leadership that wins the cooperation of others in your efforts. You have to be a salesperson, politician, and coach all rolled up into one person who communicates persuasively, with the result that your networking leads you further along toward the right contact. One executive called a board member from her former place of employment with whom she had a good relationship. That conversation turned into a referral and an interview with a local employer. Based on her initiative, she got the interview.

Another executive struck up a relationship with a professional recruiter while he was still at his old job. From time to time, the executive would help this recruiter with placement leads and other business information. Now, this recruiter could not personally help him because his search was outside this recruiter's industry specialty. However, the recruiter certainly would know of other colleagues that may be recruiting in this executive's occupational specialty or even be aware of a few job leads. Indeed, this was the case, and a little trading in relational capital produced a contact through whom he was able to secure an interview with a CFO looking for an executive.

One of my clients let his optimism and enthusiasm get away from him at first. "I can do this and that and, oh, have you thought about thus and such!" Bubbly run-on conversations that covered everything from soup to nuts were a lot of fun but they were not producing interviews. He had to learn to tone down and tune in. Sure, a great networking conversation is full of energy—directed energy. Finally, a networking friend said to him, "You make me feel like a Volkswagen with a Mac truck on my bumper honking its horn!" and he got the message. People should be able to deal with the content of the conversations we have with them and not be distracted by the emotion we create. Be interested in what the other person has to say. You are there to learn, not inform. This is not a conflict with the previous suggestion to create enthusiasm in your voice and attitude. Nothing communicates enthusiasm better than being interested in what the other person is interested in.

When you are exercising leadership in a conversation, your behavior will be characterized by listening and an energetic give-and-take around the questions you are responding to and asking. Principles similar to these also apply in interviewing situations. Before addressing the interview, however, you need to consider the next step in communicating. The next step is to make sure you are staying in front of people and that this is not the only conversation you ever have with a decision maker.

STAYING IN FRONT OF PEOPLE

Recruiters, whether they work for a search firm or an employer, have numerous positions they are trying to fill at any given time and hundreds if not thousands of resumes to review. They rarely intentionally forget anyone. The tyranny of the urgent, an occupational hazard, functions in such a way in their normal workday that a candidate quickly retreats to the back of their mind after the initial conversation if there is no obvious opening they appear to be qualified for.

This means it is up to you, the job seeker, to take the initiative to get your name back into the recruiter's or employer's frontal lobes. Many times job seekers are reluctant to call back because they have nothing new to say. The solution to this dilemma is to *find* something worthwhile to say. Expand on your USP by identifying the four or five things you do best. Then, each time you call your contact, emphasize one of those skills by applying it to the situation at that organization. Of course, when you write your follow-up thank-you note, reiterate the skill and application. This repetition over a period of time yields big results.

Let's revisit for a moment the sales cycle introduced in chapter 2: Find, Qualify, Win Acceptance, Close, and Negotiate. *Find* has to do with understanding where and how to uncover viable opportunities. *Qualify* involves your research into these opportunities, deciding which ones are worth pursuing and discovering who the decision makers are you want to talk to. The skills and techniques involved in Find and Qualify are discussed in detail in chapters 6 and 7 and also later in this chapter.

Winning acceptance and *closing* are activities that put you face-to-face with networking contacts, recruiters, and employers. You know you have won acceptance when you have passed the first hurdle and have landed an interview. The conclusion of the interview process is an offer you now must *negotiate*. These elements in the sales cycle depend on effective relational selling for their success. If you are an effective listener, are well prepared to ask questions, use questions as a means of controlling the interview, and have a ready response to questions you can expect to be asked, you will be successful in relationally selling yourself.

Negotiation will involve relational selling as well. You are bartering the value-added contribution you can make—that you have sold them on—for concessions that will improve the offer. Preparations for these discussions are presented in chapter 9.

WORKING WITH RECRUITERS AND EMPLOYERS

Recruiters and employers are alike in two things: They both are trying to fill an open job. They both have other things to do besides fill this one job you are interested in. They are busy people.

At the moment there are about 100 million adults in America. If unemployment is, say, 6 percent, then approximately 6 million of those adults are looking for a job. If it is true that 20 percent of those in a job hate the job, then there are possibly another 20 million casually looking for other opportunities at the same time. They just aren't as earnest in their search efforts as the unemployed group.

What this means is that you won't get a call back from recruiters and employers you send your resume to all the time. They are swamped and can't possibly provide the courtesy of an acknowledgment even though most would like to. It is a result of the information age and the speed of information delivery. In many cases, this problem has been circumvented by the auto-reply function many take advantage of in setting up their Internet and resume computer programs.

Here is the principle: Don't get offended if you don't hear from anybody or if the reply you get is automated and impersonal.

Whether the recruiter you talk to works for the employer or an independent agency hired by the employer, they all have a common mission. Here are a few recruiter mission statements garnered at random from marketing material on the Internet. See if you can pick out what they have in common.

> To match the best candidate to the employer's need as expeditiously as practical. (Recruiting agency)

> To provide employers the best people and products possible in order to improve retention and reduce cost of hire. (Recruiting agency)

> Professional recruitment that results in empowerment of the organization's mission. (Employer recruiter)

> Support the company's mission by recruiting highly qualified and respectful individuals that possess the same values, mind-set, and philosophy of the organization's culture. (Employer recruiter)

See the commonality? They all focus on what the company needs whether the company is the employer or the client. They don't focus on you.

It is easy to get bent out of shape after a recruiter responds to your resume posted on a Web site, interviews you for a job, confirms submission of your resume to the employer, then you never hear from them again. Though it would have been nice to hear from the recruiter regarding your candidacy being discontinued, *their obligation isn't to you.* When you finally do get in touch with the recruiter, don't share a piece of your mind with them that you can't afford to lose and burn a bridge in the process.

This is important to consider. It is far too easy to lose perspective on who should do what in the job search, take things too personally, and wind up poisoning the well. The courteous, understanding candidate will get the callback if there is a match, and the discourteous, seemingly self-absorbed candidate will get red-flagged and ignored.

When you are searching for recruiters, be sure to take a close look at their mission statement, objectives, and audience. It is a waste of time—yours and theirs—to send resumes that are outside the scope of their work.

Recruiters can be in-house, working for an employer, or external individuals or agencies looking to be retained by the employer. There are two basic types of in-house recruiters: company staff recruiters and contract recruiters. There are two basic types of external recruiters: retained search recruiters and contingent search recruiters. In communicating with a recruiter it is helpful to know which of the four possible types they are.

Company staff recruiters organize, staff, and manage a company's recruiting program, represent the company at job fairs, colleges, and tradeshows, and handle the company's classified advertising for positions. These are some of the busiest recruiters because they often have responsibilities besides staffing. They are also among the most difficult to influence on your behalf because they work with a company timeline, not their own, and receive a salary. In other words, putting bread on the table doesn't depend solely on making a placement.

Recruiters in this category especially appreciate referrals and other business information related to their overall responsibilities that you may be able to pass on as a value-added dimension of your contact. They also have more freedom to engage in conversation as you check back periodically, and are likely to be in a good position to provide you other networking contacts. Recruiters paid a placement fee are usually reluctant to provide referrals since that means someone else may get the chance to place you in a highly paid executive position. That translates into the loss of a big commission for them.

Contract recruiters are usually used as an in-house resource when the market is up, unemployment low, and securing qualified executives in a growth period really tough. They bolster a company's flow of candidates to fill crucial positions. As a hired gun, these recruiters are usually paid by the hour to source, qualify, interview, and present candidates within specifically assigned functions or specialties. Sometimes they are paid a base rate plus a commission measured against an established quota.

Your experience can run hot and cold with a contract recruiter. If your resume and screening interview hit close to the bull's eye, then they will spend time with you exploring your candidacy and preparing you for the final rounds. If you are out of the target zone in their search, they will have little time for you. It's not so much that time is money for them as it is a situation where they have been given specific parameters about the position to be filled and must spend time with those who most closely match those parameters.

Retained search recruiters are generally paid in advance by a company to complete a search for a candidate or candidates for very specific roles in the company. They are usually willing to spend more time with a candidate and encourage a candidate to check back regularly. Their income is not tied to volume. They don't have to make a lot of placements in order to make a decent living. These are the recruiters involved in the largest percentage of unadvertised retained searches for executives. Since retained searches often have unique qualifiers attached to them that a one- or two-page resume won't address in detail, it is in their best interest to explore your career experience at some length. They appreciate referrals, and even if you are not a fit for this role, they are more likely to keep your resume on file than some of the other types of recruiters.

Contingent search recruiters are only paid if they make a placement. This is where it pays off when you check out a recruiter and can discover how many present and past clients they have. Contingent recruiters with a long history of success get repeat business from those they serve and are less likely to be a candidate mill. However, volume is still key, and this presents a problem.

Employers that use contingent recruiters will often engage several. After all, nothing is paid until a placement is made. The more people that are actively looking for a candidate, the better the chances of speeding up a placement—first come, first served. This means it is to the recruiter's advantage to run as many candidates as possible past the employer as soon as they can—sometimes without really checking out the candidate's qualifications as closely as they should for a match. There are many excellent integrity-driven contingent recruiters in the business. That is why it pays off to learn more about the nature of their recruiting history before leaping into an experience that may be a disappointment for you and the employer.

Some contingent recruiters are not hired by a company. They are freelancers, scouring the job market for openings they can fill while at the same time they are scouring the labor pool for people they can entice to be hired away or job seekers already looking for work. They will present the candidate to the employer with or without an invitation. Sometimes they will even present a resume with the line "if you retain me I can get you this person."

There is nothing wrong with this free market approach. It does take a degree of cold calling, and for contingent recruiters of any type, volume is the key—no placement, no payment. These folks will be among those least willing to give you time or referrals. It pays to ask if a recruiter is contingent or retained.

Some recruiters do both retained and contingent searches, and most are very competent and professional in their approach to both types of searches. The better you understand the nature of the search, the track record of the recruiter or agency, and the different pressures they live with, the better you can adjust your communication to serve them in their effort to serve the employer.

Employers are not just concerned about recruiting, selecting, and hiring the right person. They are also concerned about cost of hiring, retention, turnover, orientation, and other human resources issues that make it incumbent upon them to hire carefully. They also have to deal with an infrastructure.

Figure 8.1 is an illustration of the hiring process in a world-class corporation that won awards for their staffing processes, in terms of both cost effectiveness and efficient use of technology to minimize time-to-start statistics. In other words, they were concerned about increased hiring costs and lost productivity owing to unnecessarily prolonged hiring processes. Don't worry about trying to determine the contents of the boxes; it is the complexity you need to notice.

Most positions in a large organization involve many people in the hiring process. You meet only with the few whose responsibility it is to interview you. Others have to be consulted; the administrative tasks associated with hiring have to be handled by still others. All of this takes place in the context of other work and busy schedules. Key people in the hiring process chain are not available, their planned-out weeks convoluted by illness, unexpected business trips, and other events. Dealing with employers requires more patience than dealing with any other kind of contact in the search process.

You may not hear anything for weeks, or not at all. The average placement cycle in a large organization for

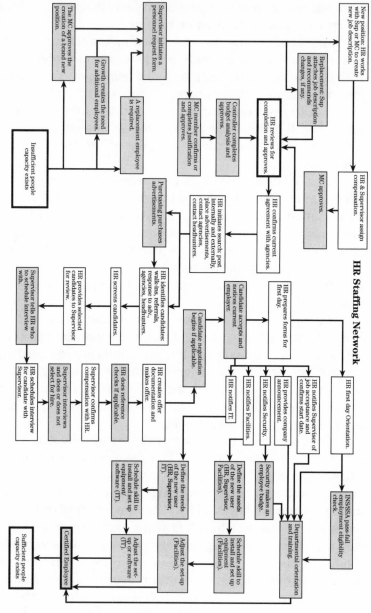

FIGURE 8.1: HR Staffing Network

an executive position is 73 days. The company represented in figure 8.1 got it down to 45 days. Don't badger the employer for feedback and don't give up on them either. The gears turn slowly, but they do turn.

THE INTERVIEW

Immersed in the tactics of a job search, it is easy to lose sight of the purpose behind it all. The purpose of all the Internet tools, self-marketing material, target lists, and networking is to develop qualified contacts. The purpose of the cover letter and resume is to get the attention of a recruiter or employer and get an interview. The purpose of the interview process is to get in front of someone with the authority to provide an offer letter. The purpose of negotiating the offer is to land the right job.

In the busyness of it all, the executive job-seeker can lose perspective for a moment and truncate the process in their thinking—a telephone call leads to a job. This is technically true. The job you land started with a conversation, be it electronic or voice, with someone. However, it is not that easy or straightforward, as we have seen. There are a number of steps involved and each has its own goals. Representing yourself well, casting the big net, developing the right contacts, pursuing leads, surviving the screening process, landing the interviews, succeeding in the interview process, and negotiating the offer are all subgoals of the ultimate objective—employment and the "right job."

It is time now to take a look at the interview process, preparing for and executing self-promotion. Earning the interview is not the only focus. You are the seller in this process, not the buyer, and like any successful sales professional, customer focus is key. Here are some tips for preparing for the interview. Some may seem obvious, but are worth mentioning:

SIGNING BONUS: DIGNITY AND RESPECT

What is it that causes you to feel as if you've been treated with dignity and respect after an encounter with a total stranger? Here are a few things you may not have thought of.

When dealing with recruiters who have tacitly given you permission to chat with them outside the boundaries of the immediate position under consideration, express *genuine* interest in them. Often it is as simple as asking them how the search is going or how they got into the recruiting business. Recruiters deal mostly with people whose sole interest is (understandably) landing a job. The recruiter is a means to an end, a tool in the process. They don't very often experience that the work they do matters to someone they cannot help. Express appreciation by showing an interest in what matters to them.

Do not ever, *ever,* *EVER* go around a recruiter to talk to the employer directly or around an in-house recruiter to someone up the chain of command. If you find yourself in a position where even the appearance of this may occur, communicate the facts quickly and honestly before misunderstandings develop. If you choose to go around a recruiter, you may be excluded from any employment process in the future that involves that company or its recruiter. Don't do it. It is shortsighted and conveys only bad things about you to the people involved. An executive was submitted to a two-billion-dollar conglomerate for a significant position by a contingent recruiter. Unknown to the executive, a colleague in a company that did business with this conglomerate was personally acquainted with the CEO. Knowing of the executive's job search, they took it upon themselves to call the CEO and put in a good word for him.

Then they called the executive to tell him what a wonderful thing they had done, which was indeed true! The executive was understandably very grateful, but then he began to think of the worst that could happen. What if word gets back through human resources to this recruiter that someone was getting into the executive office and bending ears about this recruiter's candidate? Would the recruiter think the executive, or someone at their prompting, had gone around him?

The recruiter doesn't get paid unless the executive gets placed. There is a real risk the recruiter may believe someone is trying to cut him out of the process by getting this executive hired directly by the company. Contingent recruiters have no agreement in place to protect their business interests.

The executive did the right thing. He called his friend back and, thanking him again, made sure they understood his hat was already in the ring and that a recruiter was representing him. The executive then called the recruiter and explained the situation to him, effectively cutting off the possibility of misunderstanding at both ends of the communication. The recruiter was impressed with this executive's professionalism, appreciated the call, and assured him this would not affect the process. A small gesture, big points scored. Do you think this recruiter will keep their eye out for this executive in the future?

The same recruiter told him in a conversation, "If you don't touch base, who will?" The point was that it is not the recruiter's responsibility to touch

(continues)

DIGNITY AND RESPECT *(continued)*

base with the candidate. If you have asked for and received permission to check in periodically, especially if the recruiter has suggested doing so without prompting from you, it is a sign of respect to faithfully follow through. If you don't, no one is going to call you and ask why.

Personal packaging communicates nonverbally to a recruiter or employer how you feel about them. Do you respect their professional vocations enough to be a professional yourself in presenting yourself as a candidate? Business knowledge, interview skills, and personal energy are the three "loudest" communicators in this respect. Stay abreast of issues in your profession and industry. Practice your interview skills, research the company you are interviewing with thoroughly, and have good questions to ask that will help you understand the opportunity, current situation in the role, and status of the business. Pay attention to your body language and communicate with interest and energy.

Listening never fails to communicate respect. You will find yourself listening to one of two kinds of people: left brain or right brain.

Left Brain	Right Brain
Logical	Random
Sequential	Intuitive
Rational	Holistic
Analytical	Synthesizing
Objective	Subjective
Look at Parts	Look at Wholes

Most people do both with a preference for one over the other. Active listening means providing responses and exploring comments for understanding. Practice responding in the style you hear being used.

Being assertive is a positive attribute, although most employers will disagree with this advice in one respect: Showing up without an invitation seeking an audience, no matter how brief, does not leave a good first impression. You would think a six-figure job seeker would understand this principle. Most do, usually the "gray" ones. The "green" ones can be forgetful in their exuberance. I actually had a former dot-com CEO show up in the lobby of my company hoping to have an unscheduled appointment with me gambling that his "status" would create an opportunity for an on-the-spot interview.

Recruiters face some of the same frustrations you do. Many times they are retained for no small amount of money, provide information on viable candidates to the employer, then wait forever to hear something. Logic would dictate that an employer investing in search efforts would want to maximize this resource and minimize the cost. Recruiters don't have any magic when it comes to cutting the internal red tape and may end up waiting the same 45 days you would to hear anything. Just plan to stay in front of them without wearing out your welcome.

Never underestimate the power of a good relationship maintained through networking. One executive maintained contact with a recruiter over 16 years even after the recruiter moved from Wisconsin to California. This same recruiter handled each of this executive's six job changes during that time. When I asked the recruiter how this developed, the answer was simple: "We had a relationship."

1. Do your homework. Find out all you can about the company and its products or services. Look up the latest news about the company. Try to find out who will be interviewing you. Know what is going on in the industry and what the competition is doing.

2. Plan for the interview. Be on time. Practice being positive and open. Have clean copies of your resume with you in case they are needed. Prepare supplemental information related to accomplishments, details not in your resume, references, and any other material that may be relevant or you have been asked to provide. But do not trot out all this paperwork unless you are asked for it or it is extraordinarily clear that it relates to the topic at hand *and* demonstrates what benefit as an executive you bring to the employer.

3. Practice your body language, eye contact, and demeanor. Choose the right apparel. If you have the option, choose a business suit. If they have required business casual, rather than given you the option, plan to dress slightly "up" from the interviewer. Bring a professional-appearing note pad and writing instrument to discreetly take notes. Practice speaking slowly and clearly without interrupting. Listen well. Think of the interview as a professional conversation among executives, not an interrogation.

4. Think through your answers to the most common interview questions in advance.

- "Tell me about yourself." Take just a few minutes, emphasis on "few," as in three, to describe your education or training, professional accomplishments, and goals. Go on to describe your qualifications as they relate to the job and the contributions you can make to the organization.
- "Why did you leave your last job?" This question is not designed to ferret out any problems you may have had in your last job. The interviewer is looking for a reasonable transition;

does it make sense for you as a highly paid executive? There are many good reasons for moving on. If you did have problems in your last job, be honest and circumspect in describing it as a learning experience that does not affect your future work. In other words, simply answer the question. The interviewer has to ask this question, but almost any answer is acceptable. Follow up your answer with a question to regain control of the conversation and have a better chance of avoiding a conversation that may take a negative turn.

- "Why do you want to work for us?" Share what you have learned about the job and the company. Make a connection between your contribution and their business. Show interest and enthusiasm.

- "What are your weaknesses?" Be honest. Complete the explanation with how you balance your weakness with awareness and with action that realistically accommodates and even uses this liability. Sometimes what you perceive to be a weakness may actually be seen as strength. The lesson here is to be honest about your weakness, but position it in the best possible light.

- "What are your strengths?" Be honest here as well. Having a sentence or two packed with action words is helpful. One executive said, "I am an aggressive, results-oriented sales professional who loves to close the deal. A proven coach, I have a long history of successfully building sales teams." Expand the comment with a short summary of your strongest skills.

- "What is your leadership style?" Emphasize your flexibility. Executive candidates should be able to demonstrate enough flexibility to bring to each situation, each group, and even each individual the leadership and resources they require to get the job done.

- "What kind of leadership do you prefer?" Give examples of the kinds of executive leadership you have worked under that produced the kinds of results they are looking for. Don't narrow the options by appearing to insist on a particular kind of leadership. However, if the job calls for working under a tyrant and that is not your cup of tea, be honest about that as well.

- "Do you like to work on a team or prefer to work alone?" Give examples of how you have worked in both situations.

- "Where do you see yourself in five years?" The interviewer wants to know if your plans are compatible with the company's plans. Show ambition by demonstrating you plan ahead. Focus comments on the desire to learn and grow in your field and improve your performance. Avoid casting this information in a selfish context. They are interested in how your plans will also expand your leadership in the company and contribute to its success.

- "What compensation are you looking for?" Don't answer this question directly if an offer hasn't been presented. You can always state you are looking for compensation commensurate with the role in the industry and demographic area and ask them what they are considering as a range for the position. It usually is helpful to emphasize job fit and ability to contribute meaningfully as more important to you than the compensation. Remember when you did the hard work of preparing your resume? The more effort you put into knowing and understanding the significance of your accomplishments, the better prepared you will be to answer this question.

- A savvy interviewer may pick out something on your resume similar to responsibilities this job involves and ask you to describe how you accomplished this. Some will even pick an accomplishment from each of your career positions and work their way back to front. Review your resume and be prepared to describe succinctly what lay behind the executive accomplishments noted there.

- Some interviewers will ask you for an explanation of your transition from each job to the next and probe any gaps in employment. Think through the responses you want to give. Be honest, but try not to reflect negatively on a former employer. One executive shot straight with her interviewer regarding being laid off. It was a good thing she did since the interviewer was well informed regarding what happened at the company. Fortunately, this executive avoided giving the impression she was willing to stretch the truth in favor of her own self-interest.

5. Be prepared to ask your own questions.

- Information on the company's Web site, in the annual report, or from news services may generate a number of questions related to your understanding of the company, its products and services, and the role you are interviewing for. Most major newspapers have Web sites and search engines that will enable you to search for recent articles about the company.

- "Can you tell me about your career at this company and impressions you have developed along the way?" Look for clues to the culture, prevailing leadership style, and future business development plans.

- "Can you describe for me a typical workweek in this role?" Look for clues regarding preferred hours, working styles, degree of teamwork, and typical tasks.

- "How does this position contribute to overall company mission and philosophy?" Where does it fit in the scheme of things, and does your primary arena of contribution constitute a good match?

- "What characteristics best describe individuals who are successful in this position?" Does this match what you read in the job description? Is this consistent with success factors for the company as a whole? Do you have these characteristics?

- "What other positions and departments does this position interact with?" Look for clues to how the organization is structured, how the work flows interdepartmentally, and what degree of compartmentalization may exist.

- "How will my performance be evaluated?" The answer will give you clues to the criteria performance is measured against and how often this occurs. Another good question is "What results will you expect from me at the end of six months?"

- "What makes this organization different from its competitors?" Do they really know?

- "How would you describe the culture and climate here?" This question provides direct information for several questions previously asked indirectly.

- "When would you like to fill this position?" This gives you an idea of the start date and the urgency in filling this position.

- Review the job description. It will suggest specific questions to ask about the work and position itself.

To this point, the advice is very commonsense. As a six-figure executive candidate, you also want to ask other questions—about finances, business processes, the board, the management team, market share, and business development. The important difference for you as a highly paid executive is the perspective from which these questions are answered. In fact, this can be crucial. How you talk about these questions tells the employer a lot and often determines more than the specific answer to the question whether or not your candidacy will continue.

There are two fundamental business worlds out there. One is driven by a focus on costs and profits while the other is driven by a focus on time and capacity. Both ultimately are concerned with the general ledger, satisfying the shareholders, and what the income statement and balance sheet reveal. How they get there is very different, and consequently the language they use is different even when talking about the same things.

Globalization has resulted in the integration of markets and the acceleration of business processes. The business environment can change at a moment's notice and companies most affected by these rapid changes have had to develop an ability to respond nearly instantaneously. In these companies, strategic planning takes on more of the look of project management, and the crucial metric involves what goes on inside the company. Instead of cost per product, they are looking at cost per minute of process. Emerging management philosophy for these companies focuses on time and capacity because those are the basic units they sell and the basic units impacted by rapid change. Traditional management philosophy operates on slightly different assumptions.

In figure 8.2 you will see subtle differences in the assumptions of these two general business paradigms.

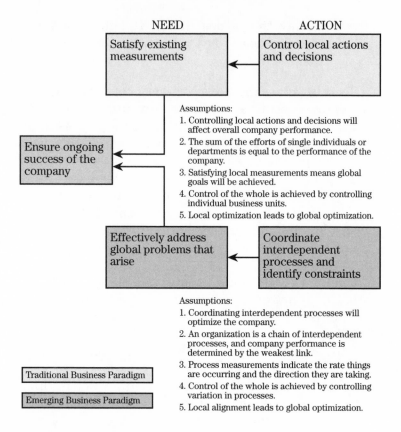

FIGURE 8.2: Changing Philosophies of Business

That is why two basic questions should be answered for the candidate early in the interview process.

- Can you describe for me the basic business process of your enterprise?
- Can you describe for me the metrics in place for evaluating progress toward your business goals?

The answers to these two basic questions will tell you if the management philosophy is oriented toward profit and cost or time and capacity. The answers you provide to interview questions need to be from one perspective or the other. Both perspectives are bottom line–oriented. However, one emphasizes controlling actions and decisions while the other emphasizes controlling processes. You will see other subtle differences. The principle is simple—learn the language of the prospective employer.

SURVIVING REJECTION

You will hear more often than not, "Sorry, nothing for you" or some other version of a rejection notice. It may be a telephone call, an e-mail, or a form letter, but they will come. If your search puts you in touch with 137 employers resulting in three offers, one of which you accept, then there were 134 employers that said no to you. Coping with rejection will become your stock in trade for a while.

Constant rejection can chip away at our confidence, self-image, and motivation. Too much rejection, and we can begin to conform to the values suggested (we have little worth), hedge in our communication (less truth about our qualifications out in the open to be rejected), and lead to overcompensating behavior (if I only try harder, it will make a difference). Rejection leads to isolation, loneliness, and unhappiness if not dealt with.

Surviving rejection begins with admitting rejection is a fact of life. Professional rejection (you lost your job), physical rejection (someone thinks your nose is too big), parental rejection (acceptance is based on performance), recreational rejection (you are picked last for the team), and relational rejection (someone doesn't approve of me) follow us from the cradle to the grave. However, it doesn't usually occur on a daily or weekly basis as it does when we have paper spread all over the labor market and the only ones we hear from are those who don't want us.

If we don't come to grips with the reality that people can be a source of pain in life, then we are ill-equipped to move forward emotionally when the inevitable rejection occurs. No, it is not a matter of sucking it up, putting on a tough exterior, and telling yourself not to take it personally. You have to face the pain. The alternative is to become angry, moody, defeated, or unemotionally logical in your response.

1. Admit it hurts! Also realize that you are not living your life for these people and move on.

2. Focus on the "real" you. What was rejected was a "paper" you that exists only in your resume and cover letter. Even then, the rejection was a matter of mismatch in qualifications; what you bring and what they want is not a match. The "real" you is a gifted, skilled, talented individual who is a match for any number of opportunities out there. You are looking as hard for a match as the employers and recruiters you are contacting.

3. Replace rejection with compassion and understanding. The rejection notice you received came as a result of a business decision, not a personal decision. Respond with a kind acknowledgment of their communication. Wish them the best of luck in their search process. How many nice acknowledgments of a rejection notice do you think an employer or recruiter usually gets? Do you think they will tend to remember you more favorably than others?

CHAPTER 9

EXECUTIVE COMPENSATION

If you were offered a job with a base salary of $144,000 when you had been earning $175,000, would you turn it down? One of my executive coaching clients did, much to his chagrin later on. As it turned out, the buying power of the dollar in the offered job's new location was greater than what it was in his current location. Not only that, but the cash value of their benefits package was almost three times what it had been. In a rush to make a decision, he looked only at the numbers and failed to consider carefully what the numbers mean.

To be in the best position to negotiate an offer you must understand terms like market rate, consumer price index, geographic salary differentials, and cash value. This chapter details what executives need to understand. It offers a refresher on the subtleties behind variable and merit pay systems, flexible benefit plans, stock options, similar jobs in different locations or different jobs in the same location, and that what is behind a base salary can hamstring your negotiating power.

TYPICAL COMPENSATION

Any approach to compensating employees is going to be limited by available financial resources. The more resources there are available, the greater is the freedom to utilize an innovative compensation system designed to support recruiting and encourage retention of talent. There are three major external influences that impact these resources: the marketplace, the law, and the cost of labor.

The most obvious limiting factor in the marketplace is the amount of profit a company can earn. You cannot pay employees with money you don't possess. Budgets for annual increases or bonuses, for example, shrink and grow with the profit a company makes or anticipates making. Less obvious is the impact of a free market economy on labor.

In America, employment is literally a bartered agreement between an individual and an employer. The employee gives their labor in exchange for agreed-upon wages and benefits. Like any contract, there are inevitably abuses and disputes. Built up around this reality is an enormous body of state and federal law that directs employers and employees how this contract is to be executed and what the penalties are for breach of contract by either party. Here is the point: Employment is a *business* contract subject to regulation. IRS regulations have more impact on how an employee is compensated than any other body of statutes.

In general, employers are required to pay the job, not the person. This is why wages can differ from one region to another for the same job and why a physicist with a Ph.D. gets paid minimum wage for flipping hamburgers at a fast-food restaurant. Of course, there are always differences between employees doing the same job—which is why most compensation systems have been developed with ranges for job categories with a minimum, midpoint, and maximum wage specified.

Competitive practice in the industry and regional labor market determines these base pay ranges. As with any contract negotiation, the employer seeks to minimize compensation while the employee seeks to maximize compensation, both using the going rates in the market as bargaining tools. When this doesn't provide enough flexibility to the employer, special arrangements are often made with the employee.

We will dissect this executive's offer in a moment. First, however, there are a number of things you should consider about base pay.

1. Is the offer for a job in the same geographic location? If you were a vice president of manufacturing in Orange County, in southern California, and the offer you have received is for the same role in the same general geographic area, then the market rates as published in current salary surveys will help you benchmark the base salary you have been offered. However, most "current" salary surveys are nearly a year old, data having been collected through July or August and published in October or November for use in the following year.

In order to understand what the competitive market rate for this job is *now,* you will have to increase the published base salary figure by the consumer price index. The CPI measures the change in the power of the dollar over time in different geographic locations by monitoring the change in prices in basic commodities. Assume for a moment the published base salary for a manufacturing vice president is $120,000. The CPI in your area for the last year is 2.9 percent. This means it now requires 1.029 times $120,000, or $123,480, to have the same buying power as when the salary data was collected.

Consumer price index figures are available online from the U.S. Department of Labor for every major metropolitan service area in the country. The CPI can be determined for various periods of time, even from one month to the next. Using this calculation enables you to evaluate on a competitive basis the base salary offered in the present marketplace.

2. Is the offer for a job similar to the one you have now or recently left, but in a different location? You will not be paid the same base wage for doing the same job in different parts of the country. This is due to competitive practices in the labor market that vary geographically, regional differences in the cost of living, and the law of supply and demand. Seattle may be paying a premium for aerospace workers while Hartford is paying a premium for people with experience in banking, finance, and insurance. Where talent is in short supply, employers usually pay more to recruit and retain good executives.

Learn to use geographic salary differentials in equating the base salary of a job in one location to its dollar equivalent in another area. Do not use the salary calculators proliferating the Internet. These are too generic and often based on erroneous assumptions. Geographic salary differential information can be found on the Web sites of most of the Big Five accounting firms. Organizations that specialize in compensation and benefits, including Deloitte and Touche, KPMG, Watson Wyatt, and William Mercer, can provide this information as well. These organizations also have their own Web sites and also are a source for salary survey information.

3. Is the offer for a similar job in a different industry? A chief financial officer in the computer industry is not paid the same as a chief financial officer in health care. Be sure you are using salary survey information for the industry represented by the offer.

When you have been made an offer, there are three things you must do with the base salary figure before comparing it to your former base salary or your new base salary goal.

- Make sure you are comparing apples to apples in the same industry; understand the differences in executive pay practices between industries.

- Bring the benchmark salary survey data for the offered job current using the consumer price index for the appropriate number of months since the data was collected.

- Use geographic salary differentials if necessary to determine what the benchmark salary data is worth in the new location.

Now you can compare what you are offered with what you were making. The executive who turned down the $144,000 offer was considering switching from his position as a vice president in manufacturing in Orange County to a position as vice president of operations in pharmaceuticals in Maine. The $175,000 job in southern California was actually worth about $125,000 in manufacturing in Maine and the pharmaceuticals industry position was actually paying better. Another way to look at this: If this executive had the pharmaceuticals job in southern California, his base salary would have been well over the $175,000 he was formerly making. Always ask yourself, "What do the numbers mean?"

ANATOMY OF AN OFFER

Figure 9.1 details an actual offer made to another executive. She was offered a job as CEO for a large teaching hospital with more than 2,200 employees.

Let's examine each element in this package, explain the offer, and explore other alternatives commonly used.

Base Pay

The base salary represents the 60th percentile of the market rate for this role in this industry in this geographic location. The employer has chosen to make a practice of paying higher than the 50th percentile, or av-

Category	Description	Cash Value
Base Pay	Salary	$188,000
Merit Pay	5% to 20% of Base Pay	$9,400 to $37,600
Bonus	Hospital—25% of Base Pay	$47,000
Bonus	Health System—8% of Base Pay Vested	$15,040
Perquisite	5% of Base Pay	$9,400
Flexible Benefits	37% of Base Pay	$69,560
Retirement	50% matching to 7%	$13,600
Car Allowance	$400 per Month	$4,800
Cell Phone	Unlimited Use	$1,200
Country Club Membership	Unlimited Use	$5,000
	Total	$391,200

FIGURE 9.1

erage, in order to facilitate recruiting and retention of key executives.

Merit Pay

Merit pay, sometimes called strategic pay or pay for performance, is a practice that rewards performance as measured against specific targets, goals, or other performance criteria. The practice is illustrated in figure 9.2. If the merit plan is funded at the level of company financial performance represented by 1.0 X (the financial goal designated as the funding trigger), the bonus plan pays 5.0 percent, 7.5 percent, or 10 percent based on the executive's performance. If company performance exceeds the goal by 20 percent (represented by a funding trigger of

1.2 X), the plan pays 7.5 percent, 10 percent, or 15 percent. The Likelihood of Achievement column represents relative difficulty in achieving this higher company performance level. In this illustration, the highest bonus levels are paid for company performance that exceeds 150 percent of the goal (1.5 X).

Now, bear with me. I am going to put the pieces of the puzzle on the table before putting them together. The degree to which you understand the details and implications of your offer is the degree to which you will be empowered to negotiate.

The funding trigger usually is some level of financial performance for the entire enterprise. Typically this is related to profit margin as a function of cash flow as measured by EBITDA, NOPAT, or FCF (explained following). Several measures of cash flow are typically used, each with different implications. You must be aware of the assumptions behind funding triggers in order to evaluate appropriately the likelihood of achieving an increase within the range promised. If it is highly unlikely you would qualify in any given year for a 20 percent bonus, you must devalue the entire incentive package by the appropriate amount. *When you ask how the merit plan you have been offered has performed in previous years, you need to have some means of evaluating how true this may be for you in the future.*

Likelihood of Achievement	Funding Trigger X	Good 2–4 Criteria (Meets)	Superior 2–4 Criteria (Exceeds)	Outstanding 2–4 Criteria (Far Exceeds)
15%	1.5 X	10%	15%	20%
60%	1.2 X	7.5%	10%	15%
90%	1.0 X	5.0%	7.5%	10%

FIGURE 9.2

Incentive plan funding ideally comes from new revenues produced by rewarded behaviors or accomplishments. The degree of reward will depend on cash flow produced by the incentive provided. To protect the company's bottom line, a minimum level of financial performance is used to trigger funding of the plan. If a certain minimal amount of cash flow is not generated, the incentive plan does not pay out.

Whatever measure is used, therefore, must represent or model cash flow as accurately as possible. This "trigger" should also be easy to understand and a commonly used measurement that is easily obtained. Typically, Earnings Before Interest, Taxes, Depreciation, and Amortization (EBITDA); Net Operating Profit After Tax (NOPAT); or Free Cash Flow (FCF) are used. Each measure has advantages and disadvantages as a trigger for funding incentive plans. *It is your responsibility to clarify in advance how incentive plans are funded and paid out—be sure you ask!*

Many companies use EBITDA as an easy measure of "cash" earnings based in part on the fact that the "D" and "A" represent noncash expenses. EBITDA gives us a feel for cash flow before debt payments, taxes, depreciation, and amortization charges reduce the income statement to a crying towel. However, it is not the same as real operating cash flow.

In its best use, EBITDA is a *predictor* more than a measurement. It doesn't measure actual cash flowing into the company and neglects variations in accounting methods, cash required for working capital, debt payments and other fixed expenses, and capital expenditures. It is an excellent means of predicting the *gross* amount of money a company expects to bring in and is very useful in evaluating financing expansions, takeovers, mergers, acquisitions, and buy-outs because it covers any loan payments needed.

Technically, EBITDA is called an unleveraged earnings measure and valuation metric. *Leverage* refers to the use of various financial instruments or borrowed capital to increase the potential return of an investment. It often refers to the amount of debt used to finance assets. A firm with significantly more debt than equity is considered to be highly leveraged. Unleveraged earnings estimates are estimates determined for a company that actually has no debt or, as in most instances, estimates determined as if there were no debt when debt does exist. It just isn't part of the equation.

If EBITDA is used on a consistent basis over a period of time, it will reflect business performance but not necessarily true cash flow. If it is used as a funding trigger, there are several things to keep in mind.

- EBITDA can overstate true cash flow by as much as 20 to 34 percent. In other words, true cash flow will lag behind unleveraged earnings measures.

- If unleveraged earnings are treated the same as true cash flow, then when EBITDA goals are met there actually may not be as much cash on hand to fund the incentive program as you planned for.

- EBITDA and cash flow are not synonymous terms even though they are used that way.

NOPAT is also a measure of unleveraged earnings. The primary difference between NOPAT and EBITDA is that NOPAT deducts for normalized taxes and an estimate of depreciation. This reflects the cash earnings a company would generate if its capitalization were not tied to debt or other financial obligation.

NOPAT is primarily used to look at profit because it does not include tax savings many companies have because they also have existing debt. However, this still isn't true cash flow. NOPAT is also used in Economic Value Added (EVA) calculations—a story for a different time. There are some things to consider in choosing NOPAT as a funding trigger.

- Interest and taxes are expenditures for a company that directly impact cash flow. NOPAT accounts for taxes, but not interest. So, even though the results are closer to representing true cash flow than EBITDA, they are not true cash flow. And there is still the matter of all those debt payments that empty the bank account like clockwork every month.
- NOPAT is a simpler calculation than EBITDA or can be backed out of EBITDA.
- Using NOPAT as your trigger will reduce volatility and the risk of nonfunding. However, adjustments will need to be made to produce a useful milestone.

Free Cash Flow puts all business activity back on a cash basis. Primarily, FCF is used to answer three basic questions: Where did the cash come from and where did it go? How much of that cash is available for equity holders and/or debt holders? How much investment is required on an ongoing basis to maintain and grow cash flow?

FCF is simply cash from operations, minus capital expenditures. This captures at least three items EBITDA leaves out: receivables, inventory, and capital expenditures (property, plant, and equipment costs). However, FCF—like NOPAT and EBITDA—does not deal with the issue of debt. It is simply NOPAT with investments deducted. If FCF is chosen as the trigger, there are some things to keep in perspective.

- FCF in effect is a means of "smoothing" earnings numbers. Reality may lie on either side of the "average" represented. If true cash flow has not varied significantly over the reporting period, FCF represents true cash flow fairly well. If true cash flow has varied significantly over the same period, FCF at any given moment in time may be wildly inaccurate.

- FCF is a way of looking at business activity as if it was accounted for on a cash basis instead of an accrual basis. This enables explanations of positive earnings at the same time the company is experiencing negative cash flows (yes, it happens all the time in growing companies). It is a kind of accounting magic that obscures the real connection with true cash flow—and it will with a trigger as well.
- FCF can be backed out of NOPAT and therefore EBITDA as well.

Do the performance of the business and the method of determining funding for the merit plans justify claims made to you in the offer? You need to know how the business functions financially. If the merit system is a simple direct-pay system not tied to a funding trigger, it is a simple question to answer. If you are going to work for a nonprofit organization, these measures are not used and the merit system will be tied to more direct nontaxed financial performance measures. Be sure to ask what measures are used.

Variable Pay

Variable pay was not a part of this offer. However, it is a common incentive method used in volume-based product/service business environments, especially sales. For exceeding operating targets in sales performance, merit pay is added to your income. Figure 9.3 provides a simple example.

1. Choose the total target compensation for the job.
2. Determine the percent of target compensation to put at risk for the job. The nature of the job determines what portion, if any, is at risk.

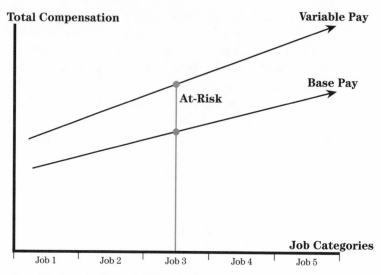

Base wage determined by competitive labor market realities. For recruiting and retention, most salaries should be in the 50th to 60th percentile of similar jobs in the demographic area.

FIGURE 9.3: Variable Pay Compensation Systems

3. Determine the multiplier by forecasting sales goals and establishing a sales budget over a given period of time. The risk amount divided by the sales budget is the multiplier.

4. Apply the multiplier at the end of a defined period of time based on collections (monthly, quarterly, semiannual, and so on).

Example: Job 3 is targeted for $120,000 in total compensation. Because of the business development element in the job, 20 percent of the targeted compensation will be at risk. The sales forecast is an ideal goal. The sales budget based on the forecast is a reasonable, but stretching, $2,000,000 over the next year. The multiplier then is $(0.20)(120,000) \div 2,000,000 = 0.012$. At the end of the quarter, $150,000 has been collected, making their bonus $(0.012)(150,000) = \$1,800$. If the sales goals for the year are met, the total compensation, including bonus, will equal the target compensation. Multipliers are adjusted when the sales budget is adjusted.

This system provides short-term performance incentive while rewarding teamwork (sales and service delivery is a team effort) and individual performance (as determined by individual multipliers). If applied to total group, division, or company sales it becomes a measure of executive performance. Since bonus distributions are a function of collections (not sales), the company's interests are protected.

If you have been offered a variable pay plan, be sure to ask for specific examples, then measure the results against overall company performance as a reality check. A variable pay system is only as good as company performance.

Bonus—Hospital (25 Percent)

In this case, this is a straightforward 25 percent of base pay if the hospital's minimum financial goals are met. Sometimes bonus plans are structured similarly to the merit plan and variable pay scheme already discussed. The important thing to keep in mind is very simple: *How much control can you practically exercise over the measures of performance your bonus is based upon?*

Bonus—Health System (8 Percent)

This is a straight percentage based on health system performance. It is vested 20 percent per year over five years. In other words, only 20 percent is paid out in the first year, the balance held for future payout at the rate of 20 percent for each year. In the bonus plan funded in year two you would receive another 20 percent from the amount determined in year one plus the first 20 percent of the amount in year two and so on. If this CEO leaves the organization, the unvested portion of the bonuses do not pay out but remain with the company. *Be sure you ask about any vesting schedules that may be associated with bonus programs.*

Perquisite

In sales environments, this would be an expense account. Perquisite policies are not uncommon ways of providing funds for expenses for nonsales executives without the burden of all the paperwork and accounting. A predetermined amount, in this case 5 percent of base pay, is paid on a regular basis to the executive in addition to other pay or benefits. This can be done on a monthly basis or some other period determined by policy. For this CEO, it will be a separate check subject to taxes paid at the end of every quarter.

Flexible Benefits

In a flexible benefits program, a predetermined amount of money is budgeted for medical, dental, vision, and life insurance and other benefits. Usually this is done in cafeteria style under a Section 125 plan where the executive can choose from a list of benefit options that the company pays for on a pretax basis. *Section 125* refers to the section of the Internal Revenue Code that regulates the administration of such programs.

Sometimes retirement- or pension-related benefits are included in these accounts and are therefore also subject to ERISA regulations. You should check with your tax adviser if this is the case in your situation. Some benefits can be attributed to you as income at the end of the year. This means there will be tax implications you need to understand. *Though this is not always true, it is important to ask about tax implications as a part of understanding the offer you have been made.*

Benefit "shopping" in this particular situation means that the cost of medical, dental, and vision coverage for the CEO and their dependents will be completely paid for by the company and will not constitute a deduction from their base pay. *This is another important issue to clarify with your prospective employer—will you as an employee contribute to the cost of benefits for yourself or your dependents?* It is common for an employer to cover most or all of *your* benefits costs while only making a small contribution, if any, to the cost of benefits for your dependents. Any contribution you are required to make effectively reduces your base salary by the same amount.

You also need to understand what happens to the designated funds, for this CEO 37 percent of base pay, if your benefit choices do not equal or exceed the budgeted amount in the flexible benefits account. Do the unallocated funds remain with the company? Are they returned to you? How are they returned to you? Only the imagination and the IRS limit the options. Ask to see the Plan Document if you are not satisfied with the answers you get.

Retirement or Pension

Sections 400 through 500 of the Internal Revenue Code are where most of the regulations are found regarding pension plans in addition to ERISA regulations. The most well known among these is probably the 401(k) savings, or thrift, plan. Yes, there are sections beginning with (a) and proceding through section (k) that all have to do with some sort of savings or profit sharing plan. There are inumerable arrangements that can be made for the executive, involving qualified and unqualified, funded and nonfunded, Top Hat or cost sharing, matching or nonmatching—the list goes on. This is another time when it is important to get the advice of a professionally qualified tax adviser or tax attorney to help you understand the implications.

For this CEO, the 401(k) program provides a 50 percent match up to 1 percent of Base Pay. However, the IRS limits employees' contributions to a maximum proscribed by law. For many executives, this is an insufficient amount to afford the savings they require for retirement and legitimate shelter from taxes. The IRS also limits contributions highly paid executives may make to such plans to ensure the plans do not become a safe haven for the well-paid while discriminating against the rank and file. This particular company implemented a 401(a) program that enables executives to make additional contributions that the company will match. The amount matched depends on how long you have worked for the company. The longer you are there, the higher the match up to 7 percent of Base Pay.

401(a) programs do not afford the same protection as 401(k) programs. To understand the risk to your investment, if any, you need to have your tax adviser explain the differences. Even though laws regulate both plans, there is great freedom to design various options into the plans. Companies are required by law to explain their specific plan to employees.

Most companies will provide a two-part retirement plan for their executives. The 401(k)–401(a) match in this particular instance is just one example of an enormous range of options. *It is your responsibility to understand how the retirement plan you are being offered operates and what risks may be attendant to the investments you make.*

Stock Options

Though not offered to this CEO, equity options constitute an important consideration in many offers. Here are some things to keep in mind about stock options and other forms of long-term compensation.

1. It is best to obtain the advice of a professional tax accountant or attorney in evaluating equity offers. Employee ownership options, traded and nontraded stock options, phantom stock programs, and other methods of providing deferred compensation all have tax consequences.

2. Long-term compensation plans can take the form of stock plans, mutual funds, insurance policies, annuities, pensions, investments, profit sharing, or some form of equity ownership. Plans can be funded or nonfunded and qualified or nonqualified for tax purposes. Determine what the plan is, how it is paid out, and how it is tied to individual or company performance.

3. A good plan will satisfy a number of basic requirements.

- Is the plan simple? The easier it is to understand, the more popular and effective it will be.
- Does it differentiate between profit sharing or commission/bonus plans and retention plans? The primary goal of long-term compensation is retention. Retention plans should not be intermingled with profit sharing or commission/bonus plans that are primarily designed to provide performance incentive.
- Does the plan have clear goals or objectives? What does the company want the plan to accomplish?

4. Determine if the plan is a qualified or nonqualified plan. Qualified plans mean the IRS carves out exceptions under which the company gets a deduction but the employee does not incur tax liability until they receive the funds at a later date. Nonqualified plans mean the matching rule applies. If the company deducts it, the

SIGNING BONUS: LEGAL ISSUES

Taxes

There are a number of legal issues you may or may not run into in the course of interviewing and then negotiating an offer. The most obvious of these is tax matters. You need to get the advice of a qualified investment counselor, tax adviser, accountant, or attorney regarding the implications and risks of the different options presented to you. This includes retirement plans, equity options, relocation packages, bonus programs, and merit pay systems.

Employment Contracts

Most employers will include an at-will employment statement in the offer letter. This is a general statement communicating, in effect, that the employer can terminate the employment relationship at any time, for any reason, with or without cause. Balancing this, of course, is your right to resign at any time with or without cause. This is a standard condition of employment and becomes important only if your offer letter goes further and stipulates the conditions of employment, including expectations, goals, standards of performance, consequences for nonperformance, and terms under which the employment relationship can be dissolved other than those provided by an at-will employment relationship. If the employer has written the job description into the offer letter instead of providing it as a separate document for information only, it is a good indication this may be more than an offer letter.

In many states, this is an employment contract. The relationship between employer and employee is now governed by the terms of the contract and is no longer subject to applicable federal and state regulations regarding at-will employment. If it is unclear, get the advice of an attorney. Employment contracts may offer some advantages, but they also eliminate many protections you have under federal and state law. Be sure you understand what you are signing.

Personality Testing

Some of the opportunities you're a candidate for will require personality testing. In general, this is a good idea. It shows that the employer is concerned about a good job fit, both in terms of work preferences and interpersonal style, in a strategic position.

Refusing to participate will usually result in disqualification, though no employer is going to tell you that. There shouldn't be a problem with completing their forms, and it is wise for you to do so if asked. Every other candidate is required to do the same, and no competitive advantage is provided if you refuse. You are on the same playing field with the same ground rules as everyone else being considered.

Every year the use of what are called "psychometric instruments," or personality tests, in hiring practices, promotions, or transfers is challenged in court. The instruments that survive court tests generally have these characteristics.

1. They are heuristic in nature, not nonheuristic. That is, they provide a moving picture of certain qualities that will change slowly over time, if at all, rather than a snapshot of something that does not represent a pattern.

(continues)

LEGAL ISSUES *(continued)*

2. They are vocational in nature, not psychological in nature. Psychological evaluations require Informed Consent—you have to sign a release and the employer must provide a disclosure regarding the purpose, use, and recourse if you do not agree with the results.

3. They are only used to surface meaningful information around which to have a constructive discussion about the job.

4. They are based on statistical reliability and validity, are socially and racially adjusted, and are not based on pop psychology or nonexistent databases.

5. Someone certified or licensed to do so administers them.

6. You are provided, in advance, with information regarding what the instrument assesses, why it is needed, and how the information is to be used.

7. Results reveal tendencies, preferences, patterns, and trends and do not identify polar responses (good/bad, right/wrong, pass/fail).

8. You are given a copy or summary of the results. Ideally, someone should go over them with you and allow you to comment.

How a company handles this dimension of the interviewing process, if they use testing at all, will give you insight into their level of competence and professionalism. Be sure you ask for a copy or summary of the results—don't just assume they will be automatically provided.

Noncompete Agreements

Many companies will require executives to sign a noncompete agreement when they join the organization. The fact that these are unenforceable in many states does not stop employers from requiring your signature. Normally, they will require you to refrain from working for a competitor for a specified amount of time within a certain distance from their operational centers. If this is a requirement of your employment, be sure you understand the implications. This may be another matter to take up with an attorney.

Signing Bonuses

These are used most often with technical positions. Sometimes an employer will offer executive signing bonuses in lieu of a relocation package. The anticipation on the part of the employer is that you will use these funds for relocation. In this case, the tax obligations are your responsibility. Be sure to calculate the after-tax amount that will be at your disposal—is it enough to fund your relocation?

Sometimes signing bonuses are paid in parts over time as a means of ensuring retention—so much upon accepting the offer, so much after six months, so much at your first-year anniversary. If you are offered a signing bonus, be sure to ask about its distribution.

employee picks it up as income, and vice versa. The IRS determines the structure of qualified plans. The structure of nonqualified plans is only limited by creativity.

    5. Determine if the plan is a funded or nonfunded plan. The employee incurs tax liability for income when they receive full rights to take possession.

Other Benefits

The cell phone, a car allowance, a country club membership are all nice incentives. Employers generally can deduct the cost of business expenses provided as benefits under Section 162 of the IRC. This isn't strictly true in every case, but the point to consider in negotiating your offer is that some of these nice incentives are not out of reach or unreasonable.

NEGOTIATING OFFERS

The first step in negotiating an offer is to understand the offer. The second is to understand how this organization is going to measure you and how much control over results you really have. Some companies focus on profit and cost while others focus on time and capacity. These are two very different views of producing results (see figure 9.4).

    There is an old adage that says "Tell me how you will measure me and I will tell you how I will perform." This leads to two very important questions regarding your offer:

    1. What results am I accountable for?

    2. How will progress toward these results be measured?

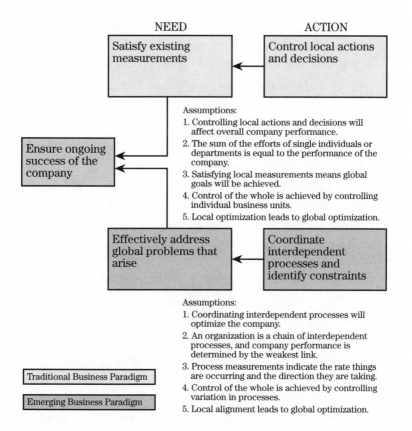

NEED ACTION

Satisfy existing measurements ← Control local actions and decisions

Assumptions:
1. Controlling local actions and decisions will affect overall company performance.
2. The sum of the efforts of single individuals or departments is equal to the performance of the company.
3. Satisfying local measurements means global goals will be achieved.
4. Control of the whole is achieved by controlling individual business units.
5. Local optimization leads to global optimization.

Ensure ongoing success of the company

Effectively address global problems that arise ← Coordinate interdependent processes and identify constraints

Assumptions:
1. Coordinating interdependent processes will optimize the company.
2. An organization is a chain of interdependent processes, and company performance is determined by the weakest link.
3. Process measurements indicate the rate things are occurring and the direction they are taking.
4. Control of the whole is achieved by controlling variation in processes.
5. Local alignment leads to global optimization.

Traditional Business Paradigm

Emerging Business Paradigm

FIGURE 9.4

If there is not agreement on these two important issues, the details of the offer are unimportant. You and the organization are set up for disappointment.

Usually, he who mentions money first loses. Let them bring up the matter. When they do, here are some ground rules for negotiating.

1. If the offer is too low, say so. If you are asked what you are looking for, simply state that you are looking for a six-figure package commensurate with your

experience that is competitive in the marketplace. Go on to affirm you would like to evaluate the entire package before providing a definitive response.

2. Evaluate the total package including benefits and bonuses or other incentives. You may need to ask for more information in this regard.

3. Avoid generalizations. Ask specific questions, get the facts, and provide specific answers.

4. Offer creative alternatives. Employers often have great freedom in structuring compensation packages.

5. Avoid emotionally laden terminology: "I *can't* consider anything less." "*No one* would consider that as a realistic offer." Emphatic statements come across as demands. You can say no without being emphatic.

6. Build on common ground. Focus on developing the discussion based on what is acceptable. This communicates interest and a willingness to engage in dialogue.

7. Use truth concessions. If an arrangement won't work, tell them why. They may have a creative alternative up their sleeve.

8. Actively listen—two ears, one mouth. Ask questions for clarification.

9. At the right time, probably toward the end of the discussion, ask for the offer in writing if it has not already been provided.

10. Don't commit immediately. Be positive, let them know that you are encouraged with the offer and that you will get back to them within a reasonable (short) amount of time. This allows you to do your homework, especially if relocation is involved.

Once you understand the offer, what is expected of you, and how your performance will be measured, you can negotiate from a position of strength.

Relocation Issues

Relocation may be a part of the offer extended to you. Evaluating relocation presents special challenges. Do your homework. Research the new location thoroughly regarding quality of life, schools, cost of living, transportation, housing, and other matters that will be important to you. Here are some questions to ask about relocation.

1. Are moving costs covered for a "hands-free" move (that is, they pack, ship, and unpack)?

2. Are interim housing and transportation costs covered? How? (Certain forms of relocation compensation have tax consequences for the employee.) Are there any tax consequences?

3. How many house-hunting trips will the company pay for? for how many members of the family?

4. Will the company or a relocation service hired by the company handle the move?

5. Will the company underwrite selling costs at origination and closing costs at destination? to what degree and in what manner?

6. Will the company buy your house if it does not sell in a reasonable and predetermined proscribed amount of time?

7. If I am itinerating the job prior to moving, will the company pay for temporary housing and transportation?

8. Is a temporary housing allowance provided while waiting for delivery of household goods?

Only a very few companies provide all these services. Most companies provide some services. A few companies leave relocation up to the employee in every respect, including financial. If you choose to relocate yourself, your reasons for doing so should be very compelling. Just make sure you get all the facts before you take the plunge and accept an offer.

In some cases, relocation packages may contain benefits that can be attributed to you as income. Make sure you ask what part, if any, of your relocation package represents a taxable benefit you will be responsible for.

Separation Packages

These used to be called "Golden Handcuff" policies. Due to competitive changes in the executive marketplace, IRS rulings, and failure of retention bonuses as a compensation practice to truly retain executives in volatile markets, most of these kinds of plans have disappeared. Instead, retention goals are more often met through the use of long-term incentives and deferred compensation.

One element has remained—the separation package. Since six-figure jobs don't grow on trees, most executives are concerned about the probability of having to search yet again for another highly paid position. So much so, it is prudent to ask about separation packages. If you were to be asked to leave the organization and were not fired for malfeasance or if you voluntarily resigned, what support will the company commit to giving you then that will encourage you to join them now?

There are two common practices: salary and benefits continuation and paid outplacement support. These are sometimes offered independently of each other, sometimes together. Many companies will continue an executive's salary and benefits for a period of one year, the gross amount diminished by any outside income they receive during the period covered by the separation policy. Outplacement support usually takes the form of a retained executive coaching firm engaging the executive at the expense of the company, the idea being that the sooner this displaced executive can find a new job, the sooner salary and benefits continuation can be ended. Many companies do nothing. There is no reason you should not ask any employer to consider making a separate package part of your offer.

Counteroffers

Sometimes your current employer will make a counteroffer once it is known you plan to depart. There are a number of things to consider before you respond.

1. Accepting a counteroffer can be risky. It will change the nature of your relationship with the employer. The employer may more carefully consider future advancement opportunities for you.

2. If your decision to accept another offer was based in careful consideration of your developing career, you may want to evaluate the details of the counteroffer and whether or not it addresses these career considerations.

3. Explore their reasons for making the counteroffer. Do they make sense to you, or is your employer more concerned about the financial impact of your absence? In other words, do they have their best interests *and* your best interests in mind or just theirs?

4. How will accepting a counteroffer affect your relationship with the recruiter and hiring company involved? Is this a bridge you want to risk burning?

CHAPTER 10

PURSUING YOUR CAREER

S ome executives find themselves settling into a career path that seems like a perfect fit in the early
years. A few changes in employers they work for
come along by virtue of efforts others have made to recruit them away from their current employer or strategic career moves they have made, but by and large they
still find themselves in the same industry niche they
started out in years earlier. Some may find themselves
in the enviable position of working in a business largely
protected from economic ups and downs, and layoffs
have been uncommon or nonexistent in their chosen
field. Yet somehow the joy has gone out of work.

This specific illustration provides an example for all
of us, more clearly seen here because of the unique circumstances. We can get fed up with what we do. It may
be changes in the way business is done. It may be
changes in ourselves as we have matured and developed
greater gifts and talents. Whatever the reason, it can
be a slow and pervasive condition that creeps up on us

unawares until one day we realize the job is no longer rewarding.

Because all the positive signs are there—a good job we can do well, a relatively secure position, the respect of peers that our knowledge and extensive experience provides—the need for a change in our career is not obvious. In fact, we have probably stopped pursuing our career a long time ago. Feeling bad about your work when there is no apparent reason can actually be a good thing.

Pursuing your career is a lifelong process, not an event that occurs first right out of school and then recurs only when a job change becomes necessary.

I first became aware of this principle nearly 12 years into my own career. In the military and in industry I had always been involved in technical roles of growing responsibility. One day I found myself not liking my job even though I was very successful as an engineer. Feeling bad about my work was actually a good thing. It initiated a personal journey that helped me understand at that point in my life that people were far more interesting than machines. After some retooling, it launched another career in human resources as well as a writing career. Paying attention to the signals since then has drawn me through many wonderful experiences in seven different industries with one thing in common: helping others to be successful. Here are a few ways you can actively pursue your career as well.

STAY INFORMED

A friend called me recently with surprising news. She had moved to the high desert almost a year ago to take a highly paid job in the computer industry. That morning after she had arrived at work an announcement was made to her: "We are downsizing and you are out of a job." Having recently purchased a home and not much else going on businesswise in the region, she was faced with making a dramatic change. This meant selling the house, looking for another job, and moving to a more populous area because that was in all likelihood where the next job could be found. The six months' salary and benefits continuation didn't seem to be much help.

With so many resources available to us via the Internet these days, it would have been a simple task for this executive to track her industry sector. Industry trends and even specific company performance, including of private companies, is easily accessible as public information.

What this executive would have learned, had she monitored this, was that the market for her particular product mix was softening. This company's customers, concerned about the impact of trade agreements bringing foreign competition into the market at a time when inventories were high following the recent economic boom, were holding their breath. Orders were being pushed out, decreased in quantity, or canceled altogether.

Regional unemployment in the industry had been creeping up over the same 18-month period of time. Knowing the status of her own organization and trends in their industry niche and tracking regional labor statistics would have clearly signaled the possibility that it was high time to be considering other options!

As I probed for more detail, I learned that all had not been well in Paradise for a while. There were conflicts with her subordinates and apparently unreasonable performance expectations on the part of the board that colored her record. The sophistication and style she brought with her to the workplace was out of sync with the prevailing culture in a family business gone public—but still run by the family with all of the attendant politics.

Most of us have sensitive antenna and can intuitively, and fairly accurately, get a read on the political climate in the workplace. It is probably a function of little things observed somewhat unconsciously that emerge in our thinking as a feeling or sense of things.

But there are a number of specific clues that will give you a clearer picture of which way the winds are blowing.

Who has left the company recently and why? (You can always call them at home.) Has there been a change in management? Has there been a change in policy or practice? What is morale like? Perhaps if this executive had compared notes with a few well-placed colleagues, she might have seen the handwriting on the wall. In my experience, when an employee is becoming uncertain about his or her future with a company, there's a very good chance that the company is becoming uncomfortable with the employee. It's a good idea to listen to the warning and warm up the job search war chest.

STAY IN TOUCH WITH YOUR NETWORK

You certainly plan to write a thank-you note to everyone you talked to in the course of your job search, letting him or her know the good news. Is this the last time they will hear from you?

The computer executive just mentioned had contacted me because I was previously involved in her placement. Obviously, one of the first things I recommended was getting in touch with her network immediately. She had done the same kind of diligent and thorough work building a network when previously unemployed that has been discussed at length in this book—and she made a startling discovery.

Enough time had passed since she sent her thank-you notes at the end of the last search (and that was the last contact she had with them) that many had moved on to other jobs and other locations and could not be reached. What's worse, many of those she did reach had real difficulty placing the name or the occasion they last spoke. The job of building a network had to start all over again.

As mentioned earlier in the book, I keep what I call a Life List. These are colleagues, friends, and acquaintances that I intentionally want to stay in touch with. This is neither purely selfish nor purely altruistic. There are many reasons.

- We share common interests and common industry involvement.
- We have worked together in the past.
- They are very knowledgeable and know lots of other people that are knowledgeable as well.
- Previous networking experience was helpful and enjoyable for both of us.
- I like them.
- They have taken the initiative to stay in touch with me.
- I have benefited from their wisdom and experience.
- They have a good sense of trends in their industry.
- We have referred business to each other in the past.
- They have made a value-added contribution to my life or work.

There may be many reasons beyond these for staying in touch with someone. This is just a place to start in deciding what criteria you want to use in creating your own Life List. The point is simple: Each week I call one or two people on my life list just to stay in touch. It means they hear from me every couple of months and then just briefly. Many of them take the initiative to call me before I have a chance to get in touch with them. Now I have an active network just sitting there ready to respond on a moment's notice.

This is a planned intentional activity you must add to your repertoire if you are going to stay connected and prepared for an unplanned need to network once again.

STARTING AGAIN

Many successful executives have not had to look for a new job in years. I receive numerous phone calls from accomplished professionals who are ready for a new challenge or have recently lost their job after many years. The normal comment goes something like this: "I have not had to prepare a resume in years. I don't have a clue how to do it." Although I think it is a smart idea to always have your resume current, the point here is that you at least need to keep your resources up to date.

Now that you have learned about several different resume types and forms of presentation, you know the mechanics of putting a resume together. So the practical aspect of resume creation is a known quantity. However, the content is the open question.

As usual, let's back into this. The challenge in putting together a resume is that you don't have the information you need. And you don't have the information you need because all of those years you were successfully performing on the job you didn't record your accomplishments. So, the answer to this dilemma is easy. Track all of your accomplishments throughout your work history—a work diary.

This does not have to be elaborate—just accurate. I know people who use simple spiral notebooks. They keep a running record of all of their activities. They take this notebook with them wherever they go so that they can record ideas, sketch concepts, jot down observations, or doodle. It's simple to enter the date before you begin your recording. And it's easy to accent accomplishments by using a highlighter.

Then, when it's time to prepare a new resume, all they have to do is turn through the pages and look for the highlighted accomplishments. It serves as a snapshot of a particular instant in time.

When you take a picture of someone or some event or at least are there when the event is being recorded, you can look at the picture later and replay the memory. However, if you look at a photo taken when you weren't present, it is simply a two-dimensional record that contains only the content you can see. You may have experienced this in another way. When you look at photographs of people you know, you see personalities, facial expressions, humor, laughter, tears, and emotions. When you look at photos of people you don't know, all you see is a picture, however interesting it may be. It is flat, without the energy that comes from personal experience and involvement.

Your notebook, just like a photograph, stirs your memory and causes you to replay the experience. Even if you have not written down every detail, your notes will probably activate your memory so that you can properly record your results.

Of course, today some people will prefer to use their laptop computers and PDAs for this purpose. I don't think it's a good idea to keep this record in your desktop computer at work because you want to be sure it will always be available to you.

I know of one person who creates a list of projects to be done along with dates and pertinent information. When the project is complete he simply records the results right on this same list, files it away, and keeps it for his permanent record.

Some of the important things to keep track of are:

- Position titles you held
- Responsibilities for each position
- Organizational charts and where you fit in
- Projects completed and results obtained
- People involved in each project and observations regarding their behavior, responsibility, effectiveness, and cooperation
- Short description of the purpose of a project, its scope, challenges faced, and how these challenges were resolved

This type of activity is easier for some people than others. Try to find some process that will work for you even if it is just throwing all of your records into a cardboard box, labeling the date range and storing the boxes on a shelf in your garage. You may never need these records but it is far better to have them and not need them than to need them and not have them.

THE NEXT STEPS

You may have learned as a result of working through this process that you should be doing something totally different with your life from what you are presently doing. However, your reality is that you have to get a job to pay your bills. This is perhaps one of the greatest frustrations a person can feel. You have worked hard to understand who you are, what you are good at doing, and what you are called to accomplish with your life. You have distilled all of your life experiences, research, contemplations, and reflections into a concise one-sentence life purpose statement. You are motivated, energized, and directed to change your life and maybe even change the world. And then, the telephone rings and your life is brought abruptly back to your reality—you need a job. You have bills to pay. You have to get real. It's at this turning point that you will make a decision that will alter the course of your life. Either you will reach for the brass ring that will move you toward real fulfillment in your life or you will acquiesce to life as you know it. And it really is your choice. And the choice you make will impact not only you but everyone around you.

As a young boy I observed how miserable my father was in his work. My earliest recollection is how he dreaded going to work and how he complained about his work. Because he was an utterly dedicated and committed husband and father and a faithful and loyal employee, he fulfilled his responsibility without fail—and also without joy.

As a young man he had wanted to become an electrical engineer. Unfortunately, he grew up during the depression, and the family did not have the resources for the expense of an education. Even more unfortunately, he had no one around him to nurture his dream—no one to encourage him, to explore options with him, to challenge him. And so he went to work doing whatever he could do, as so many people did then.

What a waste of talent. As I look back now with the advantage of mature insight, I realize how talented he was—what a creative, inventive mind he was blessed with. A few years ago he passed away, and we bought the family home. As we went through the process of sorting out the 57-year accumulation of household items, we were amazed at all the clever inventions we found everywhere we looked. His home was an archive of ingenuity. What contribution might he have made to the world had he pursued his dream? We will never know.

One impact of his decision we do know. It influenced the course for my life. When I observed how much time my father spent at work and how miserable he was, I vowed I would never continue to work at something that made me miserable. Whether this was a good decision or not only time will tell, but my father's choice influenced my choices.

And so, my questions for you today are as follows:

What choice will you make for your life?

What will you do with the new information you have about your life?

Will you give up and give in?

Will you set a new course to achieve a new result?

How will the choices you make in your life today affect the lives of your family members now and in the future?

At the end of your life, will you be able to say "I saw the dream and gave it everything I had"?

Theodore Roosevelt said it best:

It is not the critic who counts: not the man who points out how the strong man stumbles or where the doer of deeds could have done better. The credit belongs to the man who is actually in the arena, whose face is marred by dust and sweat and blood, who strives valiantly, who errs and comes up short again and again, because there is no effort without error or shortcoming, but who knows the great enthusiasms, the great devotions, who spends himself in a worthy cause; who at best knows, in the end, the triumph of high achievement, and who, at worst, if he fails, at least he fails while daring greatly, so that his place shall never be with those cold and timid souls who knew neither victory nor defeat.

If you decide that you want to pursue your dream you may, in fact, need to get a job now to pay your bills. That's all right. That's responsible. But don't let this keep you from moving toward your goal.

Start by clearly defining your dream. Do it in great detail. Use words, pictures, sketches, models, or whatever you need to make it as real as possible.

Engage your family members in the process. Help them to share your dream and understand the benefits to them of your accomplishing this goal. The pursuit of your dream will affect them, too, so it is vital that they "own" the dream with you.

The process you have gone through in this book has given you a good picture of your present situation. It's important for you to know clearly where you are now—so if you haven't done this work yet, do it now.

Now develop a plan for getting from where you are now to where you want to be. What steps do you need to take? What resources do you need? What education or training is required? Where can you get that training?

How much will it cost? Where will you need to live? Who do you need to help you?

Organize your plan in a step-by-step fashion. Estimate the amount of time each step will take. When will you start? When will you complete each step? Build in some flexibility because plans rarely work as well as we would like them to work.

Plan some intermediate rewards. What will you do to reward you and your family when you complete step one? What fun thing can you do after you complete step two? Where can you go after you complete step three? And so on. Benchmark rewards keep you and your family involved in the adventure.

And remember, you are not alone. Be willing to ask for help. You have a network in place that can provide valuable insight as you move forward. Deliberately surround yourself with positive people who believe in your dream and can help you get there. One of the toughest things you will have to deal with is people who will try to steal your dream. Unfortunately, many times these are family members. They may be doing this because they want to "keep you from getting hurt." But they also may simply be envious that you have the courage to do what they have not been able to do. This is why it is so important to find people who are objective and supportive.

And finally, remember the famous words of Winston Churchill: Never give up. *Never give up! NEVER GIVE UP!!*

APPENDIX

MECHANICS AND ARTISANS

Many years ago, I watched a mechanic in our plant use tin snips to cut sheet metal to the right size to be attached to a machine needing repair. It was a simple operation. Later that day, I watched the same mechanic put the finishing touches on a metal sculpture to be placed in the lobby.

These same shears did more than just cut. They bent, creased, rubbed, scored, and checked the metal as it was worked into something impressively beautiful. I learned a valuable lesson that day. The usefulness of a tool depends on the mechanic—and this mechanic was an artisan.

The Internet is like that. It can be an excellent window on the world, providing interactive communication. Or, it can be a work of art producing the best job leads and contacts of any search tool in your arsenal. The following ten tips illustrate the mechanics of being an artisan:

1. Most six-figure executives find six to eight favorite Web sites they post their resumes to and search regularly. They should additionally post on three to four times that number of employer, recruiter, and employment sites they do not plan to search often. This helps to

ensure wider exposure to a largely passive audience. Choose these sites carefully. Most will have information on the home page describing who visits the site and how often. It is a common practice for those responsible for recruiting and selection to keep a ready file of likely candidates for positions that might open in the near future, giving them a leg up on the employment process. The goal is to get into these temporarily passive files.

2. Every three to four weeks delete and repost your resume on your favorite sites. In most cases, the site software will recognize the resume as "new," and it will show up in employer and recruiter searches qualified by criteria such as "new in the past three weeks." Old resumes will not pop up in a search unless the recruiter has selected "all." This is not generally used since the results can be overwhelming.

3. Use a simple left-justified resume for posting. No unusual bolding, formatting, or graphics. Most upload software will distort fancy resumes rendering them difficult to read or outright unintelligible. It's a good practice to save your resume in a text format. Re-open the resume file as a text file in your notepad or wordpad program and examine the formatting. This is what most recruiters will see—not the fancy, word-processed resume.

4. Use a "Keyword Options" section at the bottom of your e-version resume. Titled simply "Keyword Options," this section lists in one run-on sentence, separated by commas, the terms, phrases, jargon, and buzzwords typically encountered in the industry your search is focused on. Resume software searches database resumes for these words and phrases, many of which have not been included in the body of your resume. Twenty-five to thirty position titles, functions, activities, jobs, tasks, and roles should be enough. The goal is to have an automated search kick your resume out for the employer or recruiter to review.

5. Job agents, or "Bots" as some people call them, are mini search engines within job Web sites set up to e-mail leads to you based on a search criteria you choose. They can be frustrating since many are simple in design and return too many unrelated results. Take the time to experiment with the search criteria and test it at the moment using the "view" button. This runs the agent on the spot. Do this repeatedly until you are satisfied the agent is as refined as it is going to get for your particular job requirements. Some job agents will have refined search options to help with this.

6. Most Web sites with job agents will allow you to set up more than one agent. Set up as many as you can. Use a single keyword or phrase in each that is different but related. Multiple keywords and phrases on a single agent will often broaden the search. Overlap the search criteria used in each agent. This will help eliminate the fluff.

7. Search engines can be your best friends. Your home page probably has one and there are dozens of independent search engines on the Internet as well. No two are alike, so use several and vary your search terms: "executive recruiters," "executive jobs," "recruiters," "employment," "jobs," and so on using your imagination. Review the results carefully and pick off the sites you find that warrant further research. Repeat the effort every two to three weeks—the electronic landscape is constantly changing.

8. On the sites you do search regularly pay attention to the e-mail reply address on the jobs you find even when the job does not fit. Often, everything after the @ in the e-mail address is also the Web site of the employer or recruiting firm. Use your search engine to check out the site by putting "www." in front of the appended address. If the site appears to serve the industry you are interested in, submit a blind resume or upload your resume to the site. Many e-mail replies listed on job postings do not

contain contact names, addresses, or phone numbers. Often by discovering their site in this manner you will find this needed networking and follow-up information.

9. When you follow-up by phone with a recruiter or employer ask what other positions they are trying to fill. Be cordial. You may want to ask something like, "What information do you need today that will make your job easier?" There may be a colleague's resume you can send them, an article, a tip where to find what they are looking for, or some other value-added contribution. This is called value-added networking. A few will respond to this invitation.

10. Using e-mail, keep in regular touch with those that express an interest in value-added networking. Always attach something of appropriate value from their perspective. You will be surprised how many of these contacts will appreciate your interest, be willing to be a part of your network, and keep an eye out for you.

DEVELOPING JOB LEADS

1. Attend business and social events. You find jobs wherever people are. Remember: network, network, network!

2. Start a direct-letter campaign. Gather name, address, and contact information of those companies you're interested in. Then send them a cover letter and resume. Make sure to follow up in a week.

3. Volunteer your expertise. At the least, you'll sharpen your marketable skills. You may learn valuable new skills. And organizations sometimes hire promising volunteers.

4. Visit state job-service centers. Chances are, there's a local office in your area. And if you have Internet access, you can check out job openings online.

5. Attend industry trade shows. These gatherings give you the opportunity to pass out your resume and meet people involved in the hiring process who are working in your field of interest.

6. Set up informational interviews. You can find out a lot about the work and the companies you're interested in. And you can also learn how to best position yourself for a job.

7. Sign up for job-search seminars. Not only can you learn valuable lessons and tips, you can increase your network of contacts.

8. Contact friends and business acquaintances. Explain your situation and ask for their advice and ideas. Remember that most people find jobs by networking with people they know.

9. Register with your college/trade school placement office. You're an alumnus, so they'll be happy to help with your job search. And often, they have access to unique opportunities.

10. Sign up for a continuing education class. You can learn new skills, and you also get to network with the instructor and your classmates.

11. Check out employer Web sites. Many sites give you access to a complete list of company job openings. And some of them may not be listed elsewhere.

12. Use the Yellow Pages. You can find potential employers easily since companies are listed by the products they make or the services they offer.

13. Take a trip to the library. Larger branches have directories and publications you can use to find employers that can use your skills.

14. Try community agencies. Most communities have a number of nonprofit organizations offering career counseling and job placement services.

EVALUATING AN EMPLOYER OF CHOICE

Many companies state they are an employer of choice when in reality few are. Here are some characteristics of internal systems to look for:

1. A solid strategic and cultural foundation.
   - Create a compensation and benefits system that will support the recruiting and retention necessary to achieve the goal.
   - Continue to refine workflow and systems to enable effective executive control.
   - Create an environment of continuous improvement in organizational design.
   - Develop a climate and culture that influences alignment of the employee to the company and the company to the marketplace.
   - Train for flexibility and versatility.
   - Maintain clearly stated and communicated vision, mission, and values.
   - Help enable market acceptance of new products.
   - Help maintain the highest levels of quality and customer focus.
   - Help protect core competencies by promoting from within whenever possible.
   - Help ensure focus on core technologies and promote continuing R&D.

2. Compensation and benefits that enhance recruiting and retention.
   - Compensate employees for results, not time.
   - Provide better-than-average pay in the industry or discipline.

- Provide a balance of motivator (cash) and satisfier (non-cash) recognition.

- No inherent wage discrimination to undermine morale.

- Performance pay tied to company, group, and individual goals aligned with company vision, mission, and values.

- Voluntary behavioral modification influenced by compelling reward.

3. A performance-management system that rewards the right behaviors.

- Effective hiring is the starting point.

- Ranking, grading, and curve systems are eliminated.

- Human capital utilization is a performance criterion.

- Performance measurement replaces performance appraisal.

- Performance measurement is set against established criterion.

- Review is systematic and ongoing, not punctilier (annual review for increase).

IDENTIFYING TOXIC WORKPLACES

Everyone has heard of toxic workplaces. Usually the toxicity is associated with control issues or misuse of authority. However, there are many reasons why a company may be an unhealthy place to work. Here is a true story that illustrates many of these reasons.

After three months of screening interviews by the recruiter and employer, the candidate was flown to the corporate headquarters of a $500 million international employer for final interviews. Though the airfare, hotel, and car rental were covered, reimbursement for incidental expenses such as meals, parking, and gas was not offered. Almost two dozen interviews took place over a two-day period involving individuals, groups, and conference calls—too many for even rudimentary consensus management the employer vouchsafed.

Interestingly enough, no one from Human Resources interviewed the candidate. Only four interviewers had the candidate's resume with them, eleven others confessed to having not reviewed the resume at all, and only two people had seen the job description. During the two days the candidate was often left alone to wander the building looking for the next conference room and scheduled interview. One interviewer confessed they had no idea why they were interviewing since they did not get a "vote."

In the end the candidate was not selected. The reasons given included being "too professional" and intimidating the interviewers. Just as well. The candidate had decided to turn down the opportunity if it was offered. In reviewing copious notes taken during the interviews trying to determine how this lack of professionalism could have been missed in the screening process—no one gave a hint of any displeasure during the interviews—the candidate noticed a pattern.

There appeared to be as many different expectations for the role the candidate was interviewed for as there were interviewers, suggesting consensus may be difficult to achieve where there are differing agendas.

The role as defined by the key players overlapped responsibilities held by others, in some cases very closely. Some interviewers were shamelessly territorial.

Some expressed interest in personality and chemistry in open and appropriate ways while others were more guarded and less informed regarding propriety. To the point, they asked a wide range of unprofessional or illegal questions related to age, marriage, family, and other relationships. This kind of questioning will often be met with reserve depending on the nature of the inquiry.

There was unresolved anxiety regarding metrics and measurements. One interviewer expressed outright resentment regarding the intrusion of this interview into their schedule.

When asked how this role could positively influence or support challenges faced by the interviewers in their jobs, two sets of requirements emerged. Those to whom this position is subordinated were looking for a breakthrough, doing things differently in the sense of better. Those for whom this position was parallel or supportive essentially advised not to make waves.

In a quintessential reflection of the internal tensions these kinds of differences can produce, the candidate received an unsigned form letter ending their candidacy dated four business days after the interviews—and the company identified the position incorrectly in the letter, naming a job the candidate was not interviewed for. The outside recruiter involved did not know anything until another six days had passed, and then only third-hand.

Competing expectations, multiple agendas, turf-guarding, inappropriate interview questions, an environment characterized by anxiety, and differing job requirements—if the position wasn't designed to remedy these issues, would you want to work there?

WEB SITES

The electronic landscape changes constantly. Some of these sites may no longer exist by the time you have a chance to check them out. Others may not be appropriate for your search. This is just a place to start. Those that do apply might also provide a special category for six-figure candidates to register and search (for example, www.chiefmonster.com can be accessed from www.monster.com).

Company	Web Site
6FigureJobs.com	www.6figurejobs.com
Affinity Executive Search	www.affinitysearch.com
America's Job Bank	www.jobsearch.com
AmericanJobs.com	www.americanjobs.com
Austin City Links	www.austinlinks.com
AustinJobs.com	www.austinjobs.com
BestJobsUSA.com	www.bestjobsusa.com
Career Connector	www.careerconnector.com
Career Engine Network	www.careerengine.com
Career.com	www.career.com
CareerBuilder.com	www.careerbuilder.com
Careermag.com	www.careermag.com
CareerMart	www.careermart.com
CareerMatrix.com	www.careermatrix.com
ComputerJobs.com	www.computerjobs.com
ComputerWork.com	www.computerwork.com
Creative Assets	www.creativeassets.com
developers.net	www.developers.net
Dice	www.dice.com
Employment.com	www.employment.com
EmploymentGuide.com	www.employmentguide.com
ExecuNet.com	www.execunet.com
Executive Search Online	www.managementrecruiting.com
FINANCIALjobs.com	www.financialjobs.com
FlipDog.com	www.flipdog.com
Futurestep	www.futurestep.com
Garage Technology Ventures	garage.com
GetJobs.com	www.getjobs.com

Company	Web Site
Google	www.google.com
headhunters.com	www.headhunters.com
Heidrick & Struggles Management Search	www.leadersonline.com
High Technology Careers	www.hightechcareers.com
HighlyPaidExecs.com	www.highlypaidexecs.com
HighTech Connect	www.htconnect.com
HireDiversity.com	www.hirediversity.com
HotJobs.com	www.hotjobs.com
HotResumes.com	www.hotresumes.com
InfoWorksUSA.com	www.infoworksusa.com
interbiznet	www.interbiznet.com
ItsYourJobNow.com	www.itsyourjobnow.com
Job Link USA	www.joblink-usa.com
Jobfinder.com	www.jobfinders.com
JobOptions	www.joboptions.com
Jobs.com	www.jobs.com
JobsOnline	www.jobsonline.com
JobWeb.com	www.jobweb.com
Lucas Group	www.lucascareers.com
Management Recruiters International	www.brilliantpeople.com
Monster.com	www.monster.com
NationJob.com	www.nationjobs.com
PortaJobs	www.portajobs.com
ProHire	www.prohire.com
Protech Search	www.protechsearch.com
Recruiter Connection	www.recruiterconnection.com

(continues)

Company	Web Site
RecruitUSA	www.recruitusa.com
Salary.com	www.salary.com
Searchease	www.searchease.com
smartJOBS	www.smartjobs.net
Statesman Classifieds	www.statesmanclassifieds.com
TheJobBoard.com	www.thejobboard.com
TheRecruiterNetwork.com	www.therecruiternetwork.com
TrueCareers	www.careercity.com
Veteran's Affairs	www.va.gov
Wanted Jobs	www.wantedjobs.com

INDEX